THE HOMERIC HYMNS

Also by Charles Boer
THE ODES
(poetry)

THE
HOMERIC HYMNS

Translated by

Charles Boer

THE **SWALLOW PRESS** INC.

CHICAGO

Published by

The Swallow Press, Inc.
1139 South Wabash Avenue
Chicago, Illinois 60605

LIBRARY OF CONGRESS CATALOG NO. LC-73-132581

for Charles Olson
in memoriam

CONTENTS

INTRODUCTION

The myths of the ancient Greeks form the most comprehensive view we have, and probably ever will have, of the mythic imagination of man. *The Homeric Hymns* assert this fullness, though their points of view, and styles of treatment, are often as varied as their dates of composition. They are among the most important primary documents we have of Greek mythology, for they offer a first-hand view of the Greek mythographic experience at a crucial, if late, period in the development of that experience.

Here, for example, is the oldest and most complete presentation of that austere mother-goddess, Demeter: grieving because the god of the Underworld has raped her daughter, she deprives the world of her crops, she disturbs the cycle of nature, the order of the world, until her daughter is returned. She, Persephone, is returned, and the crops are restored, but a great event in the lives of the people of the earth has taken place in the process, and at the end we are told of the founding of a secret cult, the famous mystery cult at Eleusis, whose initiation rites antedate even the Greeks themselves. She is an enormous creation, this goddess of corn: her power is the life and death of earth itself, and in her devotion is an early promise of that gift that all Greeks would come to recognize and seek—immortality.

The Hymn to Hermes, on the other hand is, by contrast, very much a comic proposal. It tells of the adventures of the divine baby thief, Hermes, who steals the cattle of Apollo and brilliantly fakes innocence when caught, arguing that a baby his size is incapable of such criminal business. He is completely

1

free of moral concerns—appropriately for a god whose most common representation was in the shape of a phallic stone pile (a *herma*) that served as a boundary marker. The association with boundaries perhaps led to Hermes' association with commerce, and the hymn in fact predicts his role as patron of exchanges among men, when Hermes presents Apollo with his lyre. Yet the complexity of this god extends even beyond these mundane matters: he also served as Guide for Souls to the Underworld. Thus Hermes had a unique role: phallic, commercial, comic, a thief with portfolio between the living and the dead.

And in contrast again is the *Hymn to Aphrodite*, whose function as the leading goddess of sex and fertility is represented in a lyrical narration of her affair with Anchises, and the birth of their famous son, Aeneas. The hymn is a remarkable depiction of this great goddess' powers and charms. She enflames not only the mortal Anchises, but the animal world as well, in a startling sequence where panthers and wolves and other animals follow her up the mountain, Ida, on her journey to Anchises. She is like Circe here, that other Greek paragon of animal passion, except that behind this particular manifestation is perhaps but another image of what the Greeks called "the Great Mother," who was worshipped on Ida as the mistress of animals, and whose magnitude was impressed on Greeks and pre-Greeks since perhaps the Stone Age.

There is no constant theme throughout these *Hymns*, except perhaps the conception they maintain of a dynamic relationship between man and the gods they sing of. We are constantly apprised of the proper mortal stance, the distance, the awe, before a spectre of the divine—whether it is the worried Cretans that Apollo seizes for his priesthood; or the careful old man who, while pruning his vineyard, sees Hermes stealing Apollo's cattle; or the family of Demophoön, who blunder in on the mysterious Demeter when she is actually favoring them, and who must endure her subsequent rage; or the startled pirates who kidnap a boy and then discover it is the god, Dionysus; or even the terrified Anchises, who is offered the bed of Aphrodite. Their relationship to the divine is, of course, almost always by way of an instinctive fear—but who can hear the *Hymns* without recognizing as well the power of attraction these gods held for men? The Greeks, after all, *enjoyed* these Homeric narratives enough to preserve them, and their content became a familiar part of their civilized lives.

The Homeric pantheon was itself a sophisticated revisionist view: prior to and contemporary with the Homeric period there existed a cult worship of the Greek gods, and a cult religion whose traces are present in such Homeric epithets as "ox-eyed Hera" and "owl-eyed Athena." The Homeric tradition, on the other hand, was poetic. And while its chief function was clearly to be encyclopedic—an oral record of everything that was important that was human or divine— invention, then and now, was an inseparable part of the poet's job. Homeric myth, as we know it, was an invention or selection (perhaps even an election) of the Homeric bards, based on the roots and branches of a primitive religious system. And it was here, in their genius for it, that the joy and wit of their narrative could so transpose an earlier mythical energy into an epic tradition of such grace and strength.

The poet in praise of the divine: it is an old subject, the oldest perhaps. But nowhere in the ancient world, and where in the modern, was it done so well, so vigorously, so *happily*, as by these Greeks? The charm of their verse, their enchantment, in an age void of hymns as it is of any purposeful gods, is that we too become enthralled by their art, we too sense, even if we cannot participate in, these mythical relationships. Their attempts, as poets, to articulate the life of such spirit, are that endurable.

As for the translation, I have taken the liberty of not trying to preserve the dactylic hexametre, hoping that the status of the hymns as poems might somehow be preserved instead. I hope this will not be construed as a question of impressionism versus literalism. One tries to be the most conscientious literalist possible with the original, but there is a sense of the literal that often eludes those translators who attempt to preserve original line lengths, original metres, and even the exact ancient word order, and that is the sense in which the poem itself is always more than the sum of its parts.

The arrangement of the sequence, as well, is my own. Conventional arrangement often puts the longer hymns first. There is, however, no single manuscript containing all the hymns as an independent corpus, and I have therefore felt free, as others have, to arrange the order of the sequence to my own preferences. And this is simply according to the order in which I chose, for various reasons at the time, to translate them.

This translation is based on the text and commentary of the second edition of *The Homeric Hymns*, edited by Allen and Sikes (Oxford, 1936).

Finally, I would like to acknowledge my debt to two friends, Victor Menza, for first suggesting and encouraging this translation, and Paul Ryan, for his many suggestions and corrections. I must also thank many of my students in myth and poetry, who made this task such a happy one: I hope they will take these translations as a complement to the mythologies of their own lives.

CHARLES BOER
Storrs, Connecticut

THE HYMN TO THE EARTH

The mother of us all,
the oldest of all,
hard,
     splendid as rock

Whatever there is that is of the land
             it is she
                  who nourishes it,
            it is the Earth
                  that I sing
Whoever you are,
howsoever you come
            across her sacred ground
        you of the sea,
        you that fly,
it is she
      who nourishes you
   she,
      out of her treasures
                Beautiful children
                beautiful harvests
                  are achieved from you
               The giving of life itself,
               the taking of it back
               to or from
               any man
                   are yours
The happy man is simply
             the man you favor
the man who has your favor
              and that man
                  has everything

        His soil thickens,
        it becomes heavy with life,

his cattle grow fat in their fields,
his house fills up with things

These are the men who govern a city with good laws
        and the women of their city,
            the women are beautiful
                        fortune,
                      wealth,
                              it all follows

      Their sons glory
           in the ecstasy of youth
      Their daughters play,
           they dance in the flowers,
             they skip
                  in and out
        on the grass
                  over soft flowers
It is you
      the goddess
it is you who honored them

Now,
mother of gods,
         bride of the sky
              in stars

   farewell:
but if you liked what I sang here
give me this life too
        then,
        in my other poems
                I will remember you

THE HYMN TO ARTEMIS

Do Artemis,
          Muse,
     the sister of the great archer
                    virgin archer in her own right,
                    she who grew up with Apollo,
          Artemis
     who once hitched her horses in Meles,
               sped her chariot through Smyrna,
                    and ended
                         in vine country
     Claros,
          where Apollo sat
                    with famous silver bow
               waiting for her,
                    for Artemis

And so I greet you
     and all the other goddesses
          with this song
     but it was for you that I began
          Now,
               having begun,
               I'll do another one for you

7

THE SECOND HYMN TO ARTEMIS

This is about
            brilliant Artemis
                  her golden arrow,
                        her hunting of deer,
                  her pride in arrows,
                                    the sacred virgin,
                  the sister of Apollo
                        in his gold sword,
                                          Artemis

She loves to hunt,
      in the shadows of mountains
            and in the wind
                              on mountain-tops
      she loves to take her bow,
            her solid gold bow,
                              stretch it
and shoot off
            groaning arrows

      The peaks
                  of great mountains
      tremble
                        The forest
                              in its darkness
screams
with the clamor of animals,
            and it's frightening

      The whole earth
                        starts shaking
                              even the sea,
                                    the sea-life

She has a strong heart,

she darts in and out
                        everywhere
                in and out
                        killing
        all kinds of animals

And when she is satisfied,
        when she is through
                        watching for animals,
        when her mind has had its fun,
                she unstrings her bow

She goes to the great house
                        of Apollo,
                the brother she loves,
                        in the grass country,
                                Delphi
        she goes there
                        and arranges
                a chorus
                        of Graces
                        and Muses

And when she has hung up
        this unstrung bow,
        when she has put away her arrows,
                she puts on
                        over her flesh
                a beautiful dress

Then she begins the dances

                and their sound
                        is heavenly
        Their song
                is of Leto,
                        whose ankles are so lovely,
                Leto

                              whose children stand out
                                        the best of gods,
                              the best in their counsel
                              the best in their acts
Farewell
        children of Zeus,
                  and of Leto,
                  of Leto whose hair is so beautiful
     I will think of you
                     in my other poems

THE HYMN TO HERA

Here I sing of Hera
    She has a golden throne
Rheia was her mother
        She is an immortal queen
      Hers is the most eminent of figures
            She is the sister
                she is even the wife
         of Zeus thunderer
                    She is glorious
All the gods on vast Olympos
        revere her,
    they honor her
                 even equal to Zeus
              the lover of lightning

THE HYMN TO THE MOTHER OF THE GODS

Chant your hymn for me
        this time,
                Muse,
  clearly,
                daughter of great Zeus,
                      to the mother of all the gods,
                      the mother of all men

      She loves the sound
                of castanets
        the sound of kettle-drums
      and on top of this noise
             she loves the shouts
                  of flutes

        and the clamor of wolves
        and the cries of bright-eyed lions

and hill echoes
             and wood hollows
    she loves them

        And that's
  how I greet you, goddess,
  and all the other goddesses
            with this song

THE HYMN TO DIONYSUS

What I remember now
is Dionysus, son of
glorious Semele, how he appeared
by the sand of an empty sea,
how it was far out, on a promontory, how
he was like a young man,
an adolescent

His dark hair
was beautiful, it
blew all around him, and
over his shoulders, the strong
shoulders, he held a purple cloak.

Suddenly,
pirates appeared, Tyrrhenians,
they came on the sea wine
sturdily in their ship
and they came fast.
A wicked fate drove them on.

They saw him,
they nodded to each other,
they leaped out
and grabbed him,
they pulled him
into their boat
jumping for joy!

They thought he was
the son of
one of
Zeus' favorite kings:
they wanted to tie him up
hard.

13

The ropes wouldn't hold.
       Willow ropes,
they fell right off him, off
arms and legs.
       He smiled at them,
motionless,
in his dark eyes.
       The helmsman saw this,
he immediately cried out,
he screamed out to his men:
   "You fools!
   What powerful god is this
   whom you've seized,
   whom you've tied up?
   Not even our ship,
   sturdy as it is,
   not even our ship
   can carry him.
   Either this is Zeus,
   or it's Apollo, the silver-bow,
   or else it's Poseidon!
   He doesn't look like
   a human person,
   he's like the gods
   who live on Olympus.
   Come on!
   Let's unload him, right now,
   let's put him
   on the dark land.
   Don't tie his hands
   or he'll be angry, he'll
   draw terrible winds to us,
   he'll bring us a big storm!"
       That's what he said.
The captain, however,
in a bitter voice,
roared back:
   "You fool,

look at the wind!
Grab the ropes,
draw the sail.
We men
will take care of him.
    I think
he'll make it to Egypt,
or Cyprus,
or to the Hyperboreans,
or even further.
In the end
he'll tell
who his friends are,
and his relatives,
and his possessions.
A god sent him to us."
    He said this,
then he fixed the mast
and the sail of the ship.
And a wind began to blow
into the sail. And then
they stretched the rigging.
    Suddenly,
wonderful things
appeared to them.
        First of all,
wine broke out, babbling,
bubbling over their speedy black ship,
it was sweet, it was fragrant,
its odor was divine.
Every sailor who saw it
was terrified.
        Suddenly,
a vine sprang up,
on each side,
to the very top of the sail.
And grapes, all over,
clung to it.

And a dark ivy
coiled the mast,
it blossomed with flowers
and yielded
pleasing fruit.
    Suddenly,
all the oar-locks
became garlands.
When they saw this
they cried to the helmsman
then and there
to steer their ship
to land.
      But
the god became a lion,
an awful lion
high up on the ship,
and he roared at them
terribly.
    And then,
in their midst,
he put a bear,
a bear with a furry neck,
and it made gestures.
It threatened,
and the lion,
on the high deck,
scowled down.
    Everybody
fled to the stern,
they panicked, they ran
to the helmsman, because
the head of the helmsman was cool.
      But
the lion, suddenly,
leaped up, it seized
the captain!
They all wanted to escape

such a doom
when they saw it.
They all jumped ship
into the sea, they jumped
into the divine sea.
They became dolphins.
          As for the helmsman,
he was saved:
the god pitied him,
he made him very rich,
and told him this:
   "Courage, divine Hecator,
   I like you.
   I am Dionysus
   the ear-splitter.
   My mother,
   Cadmaean Semele,
   had me
   when she slept with Zeus."

          Farewell,
          son of Semele,
          who had such a beautiful face.
          Without you,
          the way to compose a sweet song
          is forgotten.

THE SECOND HYMN TO DIONYSUS

Ivy hair,
   ear-splitting,
      Dionysus,
is who I am going to sing about,
the great son
   of the glorious goddess,
      Semele,
and of Zeus;
the nymphs,
 with lovely hair,
      took him
from the hands of his lord father Zeus
to their bosoms
   and carefully,
      carefully
nourished him in the caves of Mount Nysa.
He grew,
   with the help of his father,
      among non-mortals,
in the wonderful smells of that cave.
Then he started
   dashing
      all over the woods and valleys
when the goddesses were finished with him,
when, with ivy,
   with laurel,
      he was now decorated
and sung about, now, so often.
And the nymphs
   came too, dashing,
      he led them,
the whole forest possessed by their noise.
Oh Dionysus,
   with all your grapes,
      farewell:

But make it possible
        for us to come back again
        to this happy season—
        and after that season,
        on into many years.

THE THIRD HYMN TO DIONYSUS

Some say
        it was on Dracanum;
some say
        it was at windy Icarus;
some say
        it was on Naxos;
                divine child,
          goat,
some say
        it was at the river Alpheus,
        where the water moves so fast,
        that it was there that
        Semele, pregnant,
        bore you to Zeus
           reveling in lightning;
others say
        it was at Thebes,
                lord,
        that you were born;
I say
    they are all liars:
        your father,
            the father of men and gods,
                bore you
                    far from humankind,
                  hiding you
                          from those white arms
                            of Hera.
There is a place called Nysa,
    a high mountain,
        surrounded by woods,
           beyond even Phoenicia,
             near the streams of Egypt . . .

" . . . and they will put up statues to him

20

all over their temples.
And they will cut you up
    into three parts,
and ever since then,
    every three years,
men will offer you
    perfect hecatombs."
        He spoke,
            and the son of Cronus
                nodded
                    with his dark eyebrows,
        the heavenly hair of the lord
            shook
                    on his powerful head
        and he rattled
                        great Olympus.
After his words
            smart Zeus
                nodded his head.
        Be good to us,
            you girl-crazy goat—
        we, the poets,
            begin
                    and end our singing
                        through you—
        and it's impossible without you,
        without remembering you
        we can't remember our sacred song.

            Goodbye now,
                goat Dionysus,
            with your mother Semele,
                whom they call

                        Thyone.

21

THE HYMN TO HERMES

Muse,
sing Hermes,
son of Zeus and Maia,
caretaker of Cyllene,
and the sheepland Arcadia,
messenger of the gods,
the helper,
whom Maia mothered,
the nymph with beautiful hair,
awesome, lying with Zeus

> She kept away from
> the wonderful company of the gods,
> and lived in a shady cave.
> Here the son of Cronus had
> the nymph with beautiful hair,
> in the early hours of evening,
> while sweet sleep held
> the pale arms of Hera,
> and where no man
> and no god could see.

But,
when the mind of great Zeus
was near to completion,
and the tenth moon
was already fixed in the sky,
and he was bringing to light again
all his great works,
she produced her child,
the very crafty,
the super-subtle
Hermes:
thief,
cattle-rustler,
carrier of dreams,
secret agent,

prowler,
and soon to show his stuff
with the immortal gods.

               Born in the morning,
               he played the lyre
               by afternoon, and
               by evening had stolen the cattle
               of the Archer Apollo—
               all on the fourth day
               of this month
               in which the lady Maia
               produced him.
For after he jumped down from
the immortal loins of his mother
he couldn't lie still very long
in his sacred cradle,
but leaped right up
to search for the cattle of Apollo,
climbing over the threshold
of this high-roofed cave.

               There
               he found a turtle
               and it brought him
               loads of fun:
               Hermes was the first
               to manufacture songs
               from the turtle he encountered
               outside the door,
               as it was eating
               the splendid grass
               outside the door of their home.
It moved along
with an affected step.
The son of Zeus,
the helper,
looked at it,
then burst out laughing,
and said this:

"What a great sign,
what a help this is for me!
I won't neglect it.
Hello there,
lovely little creature,
dancing up and down,
companion at festivals,
how exciting it is
to see you. Where did
this beautiful covering
come from? Your shell
is kaleidoscopic,
you're a turtle
who lives in the mountains.
But I'm going to pick you up
and take you home with me.
You'll be a big help to me,
and I won't slight you,
but you have to help me first.
You'll find it much better
at our house—outside here
things are bad.
Alive, of course,
you're good medicine
against the pains
of black magic.
But dead, dead
you'll make great music!"

He said all this,
then, picking up
this lovable toy
with both hands
he returned to his house,
carrying it with him.

When he got back
he took a grey, steel knife
and stabbed out the life
of the turtle that lived

24

in the mountains.
Then, just as a thought
runs quick
through the heart of a man
whose troubles pile up
and shake him, or
when you see a twinkling
spin off the eyes,
just like that
the glorious Hermes
started thinking
about words and actions.
He measured
and cut stalks of reed
and fixed them in
by piercing through
the back of the shell
of the turtle.
Full of ideas,
he stretched cow-hide over it,
and put in the bridge,
and fitted the two arms,
and stretched out
seven harmonious chords
of sheep-gut.
And when it was finished,
he took the lovely toy
and tried it out
with a pick.
It sounded terrible!
The god tried to improvise,
singing along beautifully,
as teen-age boys do,
mockingly, at festivals,
making their smart cracks.
He sang about
Zeus, the son of Cronus,
and Maia in her beautiful shoes,

25

how they talked during their love affair,
a boast about
his own glorious origin.
And he honored the servants
of the nymph
and her magnificent house.
And the tripods in the house.
And the abundant cauldrons.
And when he had sung about these,
other subjects were found
pressing in his mind.
But then,
picking up the hollow lyre,
he put it in his sacred cradle.
He was getting hungry:
he bounded out
of the fragrant room,
yet with an eye out too,
and working on a shrewd trick
in his head, like those
done by robber types
who operate
at this hour
of the dark night.

The Sun
turned his horses
from the earth
and his chariot
down
into Ocean,
when Hermes arrived,
running,
at the shady hills
of Pieria.
It's here
that the sacred cattle
of the blessed gods
keep their stable,

and where they pasture
on untouched
and lovely meadows.
The son of Maia,
the sharp-eyed Argeiphontes,
cut out fifty mooing cows
from the herd.
He drove them
through sandy land
down a by-way,
reversing their tracks:
he didn't forget
the art of trickery
when he reversed their tracks,
turning their front hooves
backward
and their back hooves
frontward,
while he himself
walked backward.
His own sandals
he immediately threw off
on the sea-shore.
Then he wove
a new pair,
indescribable,
unimaginable, they were
marvelous creations:
tamerisks twisted together
with myrtle branches.
After he tied together
an armful of this wood,
he tied these quick sandals
to his feet, gently,
with their leaves.
Then the glorious Argeiphontes
left Pieria,
avoiding a wearisome trip

by wearing such original shoes,
and hurrying, like a man set for a long trip.

An old man,
who was working
on his blossoming vineyard,
saw him coming
through the meadowland
of Onchestos.
The glorious son of Maia
spoke to him first:
"Hey, old man,
bending your shoulders
and digging your plants,
you're going to have a lot of wine
when all this comes up.
But you didn't see
what you just saw,
okay?
You didn't hear
what you just heard—
keep quiet
and you won't get hurt."

After saying such a thing,
he went right on
driving through
his fifty head
of prime cattle:
over shaded mountains
and boisterous valleys,
over flowering prairies
the glorious Hermes
proceeded.

God-like night,
his helper, and her darkness,
ceased, full,
and suddenly
dawn came
waking people up for work.

28

The divine moon,
daughter of
Mister Pallas Megamedaides,
went up to her look-out post.
Then the mighty son of Zeus
drove the longhorns of Phoebus Apollo
to the river Alpheus.
They came,
not tired at all,
to a high-roofed stable
and to troughs
that were placed
in front of a very fine meadow.
When the pasture
had taken good care
of the mooing creatures,
chewing clover
and the dewy marsh-plants,
he herded them
all together
into the stable.
Then he gathered up
a lot of wood,
and tried to figure out
the art of fire:
he took a laurel branch
and struck it up and down
on a pomegranate stick
in his other hand.
It breathed
warm smoke.
So it was Hermes
who was the first
to come up with fire,
and the way to make it.
In an underground trench
he put all kinds
of flammable material.

The flame lit
and sent far off
a great blast of blazing fire.
And at the same time
that the mighty and glorious Hephaistos
was lighting the fire,
he dragged outside
two of the twisted animals,
near the fire,
(he was filled with great power)
and he threw both of these,
panting, on the ground,
on their backs,
turning them and
rolling them as he
stabbed out their lives.

He moved from one job
to another, slicing
the flesh soaked in fat.
He fixed the meat
on spits of wood—
the flesh, the back
(the honored piece)
and the entrails
full of black blood.
All this was in place.
And he stretched out their skins
over jagged rocks
so that even today,
after many years,
they're still there
(and it's been a long time too,
immeasurably long).

Hermes,
with a happy heart,
took out the rich meats
onto a smooth rock
and cut them,

arbitrarily,
into twelve parts,
but he treated each part
as if it were perfect for gift-offering.
But then glorious Hermes himself
wanted some of the sacred meat:
immortal or not,
the delicious smells
troubled him.
His noble heart
persuaded him, however,
not to let them pass
down his own divine gullet,
though he wanted to,
badly.

He put them away at first
in the high-roofed stable,
the fat and the abundant meat,
then he held them up
into the air,
as a commemoration
of his recent foray.
And he gathered up
burnable wood,
and the blast of its fire
completely swept over
their feet and their heads.

When the god had completed
everything according to custom,
he threw his sandals
into the Alpheus
with its deep waters.
Then he quenched the coals,
and for the rest of the night
kicked sand over the black ashes.
The beautiful light of the moon
shone down on him.

At dawn
he went back again
to the divine peaks of Cyllene,
and nobody
ran into him at all
on this long route,
nobody from the blessed gods,
nobody from mortal men,
no dogs even
barked.
Hermes,
son of Zeus,
the helper,
slid in through an opening
into the room,
like a breeze in autumn,
like a mist.
He went directly
into the rich shrine of the cave,
tip-toeing.
He didn't make a lot of racket
as one usually does on the floor.
The glorious Hermes
quickly got into his cradle.
He wrapped his blanket
around his shoulders,
just like a baby,
playing in his hand
with the cloth
around his knees.
There he lay,
holding onto his lovely lyre
with his left hand.
But the god
couldn't fool his mother,
the goddess,
who said this:
"Just what are you up to, smartie?

Where were you that you come in
at this hour of the night,
impudence written all over you?
Now I'm beginning to think
you would walk right out the front door
under the arm of Apollo,
if it weren't bolted on all sides
with chains that are unbreakable,
put there so you wouldn't go plundering
all over the valley! Well go ahead!
Get out! Your father made you
just to be a big headache
to gods and men!"

                Hermes answered her
                shrewdly:
                "Mother,
                why do you aim these things at me,
                as if I were a little kid
                who knew a lot of good rules
                in his head, and could be scared,
                a kid who could be scared
                by his mother's words?
                Why, I shall be engaged
                in the greatest art of all—
                always concerned for you,
                of course, and for myself.
                We're not going to stick around here,
                as you want, the only two
                among all the immortal gods
                without any gifts,
                without even prayers!
                It's much better
                to spend every day
                talking with the gods,
                rich, bountiful, loaded with
                cornfields, than to just
                sit around home here
                in this creepy cave.

As for honors,
I'm going to get in on the same ones
that are sacred to Apollo.
And if my father won't stand for it,
I'll still try,
I'm capable certainly,
to be the number one thief.
And if the glorious son of Leto
searches for me, I think
things will turn out the worse
for him. I'll go to Pytho,
barging right in
to his great house.
And then I'll cart off
loads of tripods
and beautiful cauldrons and gold
and fiery iron
and lots of good stuff.
You'll see—
if you want to."
That's how the two of them
carried on with each other,
one, the son of Zeus,
holder of the aegis,
the other, the lady Maia.
Dawn, the early riser,
was getting up
out of the Ocean bed,
bringing people their light,
by the time
Apollo had made it
to Onchestos,
that charming grove
that is sacred
to the noisy shaker of the earth.
There he ran into
an old man,
who was pruning

                his vineyard
                by the side of the road.
The famous son of Leto
was the first to speak:
"Hey old-timer,
you there from green Onchestos,
cutting thorns,
I come from Pieria
and I came here
looking for my cows—
all females,
all with curved horns,
they're from my herd.
The bull was grazing
alone, apart from the others.
He's black.
And there's four bright-eyed dogs too.
They follow right behind.
Those dogs think
just like people. Anyway,
my dogs and my bull
were left behind—
which is what really puzzles me.
It was right after the sun went down
that my cows left.
They left a soft meadow,
and a tasty pasture.
Tell me this, old-timer,
and you really are an old one,
did you see a man
coming down this way
with cows like these?"
                The old man answered him
                with these words:
                "My friend, it's hard to say
                all the things a fellow can see
                with his eyes.
                Many travelers use this road,

                            35

and some come and go
with very bad things in their mind,
others with very good things.
And it's awfully hard
to know everyone.
As for me, I was working
all day long
up until the sun set
digging away in my
very profitable,
wine-producing vineyard.
But it seems to me,
my friend, I saw a child—
but really, I don't know,
I didn't see him clearly,
I don't know who the child was
that followed behind
those beautifully horned cows,
he was awfully young, though,
a baby,
and he carried a staff,
and he walked along zigzag,
he pushed them along backwards
with their heads facing him!"
The old man spoke.
The god listened,
then went on down the road.
He saw a bird
with long wings,
and immediately knew
that the thief
had been born
a child of Zeus.
Violently
he rushed to holy Pylos,
this son of Zeus,
this lord Apollo,
searching

for his cows
that roll as they walk.
He covered his broad shoulders
in a dark cloud.
                    The Archer
                    recognized their tracks
                    and spoke this speech:
                    "Oh my god,
                    what a fantastic thing this is
                    that I see with my eyes!
                    These are the tracks
                    of straight-horned cows
                    but they're turned back
                    in the direction of
                    the valley of asphodels!
                    And these aren't the footprints
                    of a man,
                    or a woman,
                    or a wolf with grey skin,
                    or a bear,
                    or a lion.
                    And I can't even expect them to be
                    a shaggy centaur's—
                    whoever it was that made such monstrosities
                    with their quick feet
                    as they went along.
                    On one side of the road
                    they're strange.
                    But on the other side
                    they're even stranger!"
He said this,
the son of Zeus,
the lord Apollo,
and rushed along
and came to the mountain of Cyllene,
covered in forest,
to the rocky and dark
secret hiding-place

where the divine nymph
bore the son of Zeus.
A marvelous fragrance
wafted around
the holy mountain
and many tender-footed sheep
pastured up there.
                              Then Apollo,
                              yes the Archer Apollo himself,
                              speeding too,
                              rushed over the stone threshold
                              and into the misty cave.
                              When Hermes,
                              the son of Zeus and Maia,
                              saw who it was,
                              the Archer Apollo,
                              and that he was mad
                              about his cattle,
                              he sank down deeper
                              under the fragrant covers,
                              the way a heap of ashes
                              covers over
                              the burned-out remains
                              of a tree stump.
                              That was how Hermes
                              tried to hide himself
                              when he saw Apollo.
He rolled up his head
and his hands
and his feet
together in a little ball,
faking sweet sleep,
looking like a baby
just after his bath,
though he was really awake.
And he held his lyre
under his arm.
But he knew them,

the son of Zeus and Leto
didn't fail to recognize
the very beautiful mountain nymph
and her dear son,
that tiny child,
disguising himself
with brilliant tricks.
               Apollo looked around
               every corner of the entire house,
               then he opened three special rooms,
               using a shiny key.
               The rooms were full of nectar
               and delicious ambrosia.
               There was a lot of gold inside too,
               and silver, and many dresses
               of the nymph, some dark,
               some silvery—
               the sort of thing
               that the sacred houses
               of the blessed gods
               have inside.
When the son of Leto
had finished looking around
the back rooms of the great house,
he spoke words to
the glorious Hermes:
"Listen kid,
lying in your cradle,
tell me where my cows are,
and quick!
We're going to fight this out
and it won't be very pretty!
I'm going to take you
and throw you into black Tartarus,
into a hopeless darkness.
What a terrible end!
And neither your mother
nor your father

39

will bring you back
to the light of day!
You'll wander
under the earth,
leading little people around!"
                              Hermes answered him
                              coolly:
                              "Son of Leto,
                              why do you speak so rudely,
                              and why come here
                              looking for your animals?
                              I didn't see anything,
                              I didn't learn anything,
                              I didn't hear anything
                              from anybody else.
                              I don't have any information to give,
                              and the reward for information
                              wouldn't go to me
                              if I did.
                              I'm not like a person
                              who drives away cattle,
                              I'm not big enough!
                              This wasn't my work!
                              I'm interested
                              in other kinds of things:
                              sleep is what I care about,
                              and the milk of my mother.
                              I care about blankets
                              around my shoulders.
                              And having hot baths!
                              I sure hope
                              nobody hears
                              what this argument is about!
                              And it would be a big surprise
                              for the gods: a baby,
                              just new-born,
                              who could walk right in the door
                              with a herd of cows.

What you're talking about
is ridiculous.
I was just born yesterday!
My feet are still very soft.
The ground underneath them
is pretty hard.
If you want,
I'll swear a great oath
on the head of my father:
I declare that I am myself
not guilty,
nor did I see any other thief
of your cattle,
whatever cattle are, anyway—
I've only heard about them."
And while he said this,
he peeked out
from under his bright eyelids,
looking here and there.
And he whistled too,
for a long time,
like somebody listening to a lie.
The Archer Apollo,
laughing softly,
said this to him:
"Friend,
trickster,
sharpie,
the way you talk
I bet you have broken into
a lot of expensive homes
in nights past
and left more than one man
with nothing more to sit on
than his doorsill,
looting his home
without a sound.
And you'll be a nuisance to

41

shepherds in the fields
of mountain-valleys,
whenever you're in the mood for
meat, and you come across
herds of cattle
and flocks of sheep.
But come on,
get out of that cradle,
unless you want to sleep
your deepest and final sleep,
come on,
companion of black night!
For from now on
you will hold
this honor among the gods:
for all time
you will be called
'The Prince of Thieves!' "

Phoebus Apollo
said this and then
seized him.
The powerful Argeiphontes,
lifted up by the god's arms,
intentionally
released an omen,
an insolent servant
of his stomach,
a reckless little messenger.
Right after this
he suddenly sneezed too.

Apollo heard it,
and threw the glorious Hermes
out of his arms
and down to the ground.
He sat down
in front of him,
and although anxious to leave,
he spoke these words to Hermes,

42

blisteringly:
"Don't be afraid,
little baby in your blankets,
son of Zeus and Maia.
With these omens
I'll find
the powerful heads
of my cattle.
And it's you who will lead me
on the way."
He said this.
Cyllenian Hermes
quickly jumped up
in a hurry to go,
using his hands to cover
his ears with the blanket
he had wrapped
around his shoulders,
and saying this:
"Where are you taking me, Apollo,
most violent of all the gods?
Is it because of your cows
that you're angry
and is that why you attack me?
Damn it, I wish
the whole race of cows
would die! Because
I didn't steal your cattle,
and I didn't see anyone else,
whatever cattle are, anyway—
I've only heard about them.
Be fair,
in the name of Zeus,
and I'll be fair to you."
And the two of them
went on discussing
each of their points in detail,
the shepherd Hermes

43

and the noble son of Leto,
both of them angry—
one of them, speaking truthfully
and not without reason,
seized glorious Hermes
for the sake of his cattle—
the other, the one from Cyllene,
wanted to deceive Silver-Bow
with tricks and clever words.
But even though he was himself
very smart,
Hermes
had come up against someone
really wise.
So, quickly then,
Hermes walked along the sand, ahead,
while the son of Zeus and Leto
walked behind.
These two very charming children
of Zeus came immediately
to the peak of fragrant Olympos
to their father, the son of Cronus.
Here they both waited out
the weighing out of justice.
Chuckles broke out
on snow-capped Olympos,
as the incorruptible gods
assembled after dawn
on her golden throne.
Hermes and Silver-Bow Apollo
stood before the knees of Zeus.
High-thundering Zeus
questioned his brilliant son
and spoke this word to him:
"Phoebus,
why do you bring us
this pleasant little prisoner,
this new-born baby,

44

who has the makings
of a herald?
This is serious business
that has come before
the assembly of the gods."
Lord Apollo, the Archer,
answered him:
"Father, you're going to hear now
a rather difficult story—
you who charge me alone
with being the greediest
person for loot.
This little boy here,
this thief, I found
in the mountains of Cyllene,
and I had to search hard
in many lands to find him.
What a snip—
I've never seen anyone like him
among the gods
or among the kind of men
who go about the earth
trying to cheat people.
After stealing my cows
he drove them out of their meadow
in the evening along the shore
of the noisy sea,
heading straight for Pylos.
They made double tracks—
it was fantastic, it was enough
to shake you up—it was
the work of a powerful demon!
As for my cows,
the dark dust
indicated their feet
were turned towards
the valley of asphodels,
but he was himself undetectable.

Impossible!
He didn't go
on his hands
or on his feet
over the sandy terrain,
but by some other means
he made his way.
It was marvelous!
It was as if he had used
little trees for feet!
While he proceeded
along the sandy terrain
it was easy to make out
all their tracks in the dust.
But when he had finished
with the long trek
along the sandy terrain,
the tracks of the cattle
and his own
suddenly became imperceptible
on harder ground.
A mortal man saw him
driving the herd
of long-faced cattle
toward Pylos.
And when he had locked up the herd
in a quiet place,
he jumped along from one side of the road
to the other, then
he lay down in his cradle
just like the black night itself,
in the darkness of a misty cave.
Not even an eagle,
with its sharp eye,
could have spotted him
down there. And often
he would wipe his eyes
with his hands,

cooking up another trick.
Then he spoke to me,
bluntly:
'I didn't see anything,
I didn't learn anything,
I didn't hear anything
from anybody else.
I don't have any information
to give, and the reward for information
wouldn't go to me
if I did."

        After he spoke all this,
        Phoebus Apollo sat down.
        Hermes also had a speech
        for the gods, and he pointed
        to Zeus, the commander of all gods:
        "Father Zeus,
        I'm going to tell you the truth.
        I'm a frank person,
        and I don't know how to lie.
        He came to our house today,
        just after sunrise,
        searching for his cows
        that roll as they walk.
        He didn't bring with him
        any of the blessed gods
        as witnesses or observers.
        He ordered me to talk,
        using considerable force.
        He even threatened
        to throw me into deep Tartarus,
        because he possessed
        the delicate flower
        of glorious youth,
        while I, I was just born
        yesterday—
        and he knew I was too—
        and that I wasn't like

a cattle-rustler,
or a big person.
Believe me—
you who have the honor
of boasting that you are
my father—
I didn't take his cattle home,
though I do want to be rich.
I didn't even step over
our doorstep.
I tell you this in all honesty.
I have a great deal of respect
for the Sun and the other spirits.
And I love you.
And I dread him.
And you yourself know
that I am not guilty.
And I'll even add
this great oath:
NOT GUILTY,
by these beautiful porticoes
of the gods!
And a day will come
when I will pay him back
for his reckless charges,
even though he's stronger.
But you, Zeus,
help us youngsters!"
Argeiphontes of Cyllene
said this—and winked!
And he clutched onto his blanket
on his arm. He didn't remove it.
Zeus let out a great big laugh
as he looked at this kid,
who was up to no good,
denying so well,
so smoothly,
that he knew anything

about the cows.
And he ordered both of them
to try to reconcile themselves
to each other.
And he ordered
Hermes the Guide
to lead the way
and point out the place—
without any further mischief—
where he had hid
that powerful herd of cattle.
Zeus merely nodded,
and the noble Hermes obeyed him.
For the mind of Zeus
who carries the aegis
persuades easily.

        These two very charming children of Zeus
        hurried away, and came to
        sandy Pylos, to a ford of the Alpheus.
        Then they came to the fields
        and to the high-roofed stable
        where the cattle found food
        in the nighttime.
        Then Hermes, going into the stone cave,
        drove out into the light
        that powerful herd of cattle.

The son of Leto,
looking from far off,
spotted the cow-skins
on the steep rock,
and immediately inquired
of glorious Hermes:
"You trickster,
how were you able
to cut up two cow-skins?
You're just an infant,
and you were just born!
I'm shocked, myself,

to think of what your power
will be like later on.
There's no need
for you to grow up big,
son of Maia
from Cyllene."
He spoke,
and started tying up
the arms of the god
with powerful thongs of willow.
Those he put on his feet, however,
suddenly started growing
down into the ground,
twisting together,
and easily tangled up
all the wild cattle there—
thanks to the schemes
of tricky Hermes.
Apollo was shocked!
Then the powerful Argeiphontes
looked up and down,
suggestively, a fire
twinkling in his eyes . . .
. . . he wanted to hide.
It was very easy for him
to soothe the Archer,
son of glorious Leto,
as he wanted to do,
even though he was so strong.
He took his lyre
in his left hand,
and tried, with the pick,
to sound melodic.
and under his hand
it sounded marvelous!
Phoebus Apollo
was delighted, and
burst out laughing.

The lovely sound
of this divine voice
went right to his heart,
and a sweet desire
transfixed his spirit
as he listened.
                    The son of Maia,
                    playing his lyre so charmingly,
                    took courage, and stood
                    on the left
                    of Phoebus Apollo.
                    Suddenly he started playing the lyre
                    louder, reciting a prelude—
                    and the sound accompanying him
                    was lovely—
                    about the immortal gods
                    and the dark earth,
                    how they were in the beginning,
                    and what prerogatives each one had.
                    And the first of the gods
                    that he commemorated with his song
                    was Mnemosyne, Mother of Muses,
                    for the son of Maia
                    was a follower of hers.
                    And all of them,
                    all the immortal gods,
                    according to age
                    and how each one was born,
                    the glorious son of Zeus
                    recited, singing them all
                    in order, playing his lyre
                    on his arm.
And Apollo felt
a deep and irresistible desire
seize him,
and he spoke to him
these true words:
"Cow-killer,

you who work so hard
on inventions,
companion at festivals,
this song of yours
is worth fifty head.
From now on
I think our differences
can be settled peaceably.
Come on now, tell me,
ingenious son of Maia,
were you born with
a talent for this fantastic thing,
or was there some god
or maybe some mortal man
who gave it to you as a great gift,
and taught you
how to sing this divine music?
For I hear this marvelous
and fresh voice,
which nobody else ever
knew how to do,
no mortal man
and none of the gods
who make their home on Olympos,
nobody but you, thief,
son of Zeus and Maia.
What is this art?
What is this Muse
for incurable sorrows?
Do you have to practice?
You get
three sure things from it:
you get jolliness,
love, and sweet sleep,
whichever you want.
Why, I've accompanied
the Olympian Muses
who are so concerned with dancing,

and the noble voice of poetry,
the full song
and the delightful noise
of flutes—
but my heart has never been so struck
by anything as it has by this—
not even by the sort of things
put on by youth at feasts,
Son of Zeus,
I marvel
at the lovely way
you play the lyre!
Now then,
even though you're so little,
since you know
such glorious skills,
sit down, my friend,
and listen to a word
from one of your elders:
from now on
you are going to have glory
among the immortal gods,
yourself and your mother.
And when I tell you this,
I mean it:
YES, by my cornel-wood spear,
I'm going to make you
the famous and rich Guide
among the Gods.
And I'm going to give you
some wonderful presents too,
and I won't trick you
in the end."

        Hermes replied to him
        with these shrewd words:
        "You ask these things
        very seriously, Archer.
        And I won't refuse

to introduce you to our art.
You'll learn it
this very day.
I want to be kind to you
in my thought
and in my words.
But you know everything
very well in your mind.
You sit in first place
among the gods,
son of Zeus.
You're good and strong.
Wise Zeus loves you,
and it's only right that he does,
and he's brought you
wonderful presents.
They say
you learned the honors due to gods
and the oracles from Zeus,
and all his laws.
I have learned myself that you have
an abundance of all these things.
And here too I know
why it is you are rich.
It's up to you
to learn
whatever it is you want.
And since the spirit moves you
to play the lyre,
sing, play it,
enjoy the fun
that you receive from me.
But give the glory to me,
friend.
Take this clear-voiced companion
in your hands
and sing—
you know how to express yourself

beautifully and in harmony.
And how serene it is, too,
to bring it
to some rollicking festival,
to some pleasant dance,
even to all-out revelry!
It's fun day or night!
The person who really works at it,
studying it with craft
and intelligence,
who learns to do it pleasantly,
sounding it expertly,
easily entertains
with its pleasures,
driving away
work's weariness.
But if some lunkhead
comes along
and goes at it furiously,
it's hopeless,
every note will be wrong
and struck into the air.
It's up to you
to learn
whatever it is you want.
And I'm even going to give it to you,
noble son of Zeus.
And I will have cattle
graze the pastures,
and on the mountains
and on the plain
that feeds horses.
And cows will mate with bulls
promiscuously, and bring forth
an abundance of males and females.
It's not right then
for you to be violently angry,
even if you are a bit greedy."

He said this,
and held it out to him.
And Phoebus Apollo received it,
and bestowed upon Hermes in turn
his shining whip,
and gave him charge of
the care of cattle.
And the son of Maia
received it laughing.
And the glorious son of Leto
took the lyre in his left hand,
the Lord Apollo, the Archer,
and tested it, part
by part, with the pick.
And under the god's hand
it sounded charming,
and he sang along beautifully.
Then they led the cattle
to the sacred meadow.

> Then the two of them,
> these very charming children of Zeus,
> hurried back to snow-capped Olympos,
> enjoying the lyre.
> And wise Zeus was delighted,
> and urged them to love each other.
> Then and there Hermes decided
> to love the son of Leto,
> and he still does even now.
> The proof of this is
> that he gave the Archer
> his lovely lyre
> and that he knew how to play it
> as soon as he picked it up.
> And Hermes invented for himself
> the instrument of another art:
> he made the shepherd's pipe,
> the sound of which
> can be heard from far off.

And then it was that the son of Leto
had this to say to Hermes:
"Son of Maia,
Guide,
smarty,
I'm afraid
that some day you're going to steal
my lyre and my curved bow.
You have the honor,
from Zeus, of being in charge of
exchanges among men
on the nourishing earth.
But, if you would be so bold
as to swear the great oath of the gods,
either by a nod of your head,
or by the powerful waters of the Styx,
then you would make my heart
favorable and friendly."
　　　　　　Then the son of Maia promised,
　　　　　　nodding his head,
　　　　　　that he would never again steal
　　　　　　anything the Archer possessed,
　　　　　　and that he would never again go near
　　　　　　his sturdy house.
　　　　　　So Apollo, the son of Leto,
　　　　　　promised for his part,
　　　　　　in bond and friendship,
　　　　　　that there never would be
　　　　　　anyone else among the immortals
　　　　　　that he would love more,
　　　　　　whether it was a god
　　　　　　or just a man born of Zeus.
"I am going to make of you
a symbol
among immortals and everybody else,
and you will be trusted
and honored in my heart.
Furthermore,

I'm going to give you
a marvelous wand
for fortune and wealth,
made of gold and triple-leafed,
and it will keep you safe
when you are carrying out
all the decrees
of favorable words and actions
which I say I know
from the voice of Zeus.
But as for oracles,
my dearest friend,
which you are always asking about,
it isn't permitted for you
to know them,
nor any other god.
For the mind of Zeus alone
knows them.
I have given my word
and sworn a strong oath
that nobody other than myself
among the ever-living gods
shall know
the profound will of Zeus.
And so,
my brother now in the golden wand,
do not ask me
to reveal the divine secrets to you
which far-seeing Zeus contemplates.
I shall harm some men,
help others,
bothering many
of the race of unenviable mankind.
And some will profit
from my voice:
those who hearken
to the cry and the flights
of prophetic birds.

These men will profit
from my voice—
I won't deceive them.
But to those who believe in
birds that just chatter,
and want to question my oracles
against my will,
in order to know more
than the ever-living gods,
I say this:
they're on the wrong track,
even though I accept their gifts.
And I have something else to tell you,
son of glorious Maia
and of Zeus who carries the aegis,
you who are the helper spirit
of the gods.
For there are some Fates,
three of them,
sisters by birth,
virgins
who take pleasure in their swift wings.
Their heads have been sprinkled over
with a white barley-powder.
They make their homes
under the cliffs of Parnassus.
They taught divination
independent of me, while I
was still a child practicing it
around my cattle.
My father didn't stop them.
From there, they
fly, now here,
now there,
and eat beeswax
and accomplish everything.
And when they have been fed
on the golden honey,

they are inspired
and want to pronounce truths,
all of their own accord.
If, however,
they are kept away from
this sweet food of the gods,
then they try to lead you astray.
Well, I give them to you.
And if you ask them something sincerely,
rejoice over it.
And if you teach some mortal man,
he will hear you—
if he is lucky.
Take these things,
son of Maia,
and the rustic cattle
that roll as they walk,
and take care of horses,
and hard-working mules."
And over bright-eyed lions
and white-tusked pigs,
over dogs and sheep
who nourish the wide earth,
over all the animals,
it's for the glorious Hermes
to rule, and to be
the only recognized messenger
to Hades, who himself
never takes a gift from anybody.
This time, though, he will give him
a gift that is far from least.
       And that's how
       the lord Apollo
       came to love the son of Maia,
       with many signs of friendship,
       and the son of Cronus
       added his favor.
       And Hermes mingles now

with all men and gods.
And even though
he helps a few people,
he cheats an endless number
of the race of mortal men
in the darkness of night.

So then,
son of Zeus and Maia,
farewell!
But I will think of you
in my other poems.

THE SECOND HYMN TO HERMES

This song
is to Hermes of Cyllene:

                killer of Argos,
                ruler of Cyllene
                and the sheep-land, Arcadia
                messenger of the gods
                the helper.

Maia became his mother,
    (she was awesome)
        the daughter of Atlas,
            after she made love
                    with Zeus.

She kept away from the crowd
    of happy gods,
        and lived in a dark cave.

It was there that Zeus went,
    in the middle of the night,
        to make love
            to the nymph with beautiful hair
                while sweet sleep
                    held the pale arms of Hera.

It all escaped the notice
    of the immortal gods
        and mortal men.

Hail to you,
        son of Zeus and Maia.

I began this hymn
        for you
and now I will pass on
        to another hymn.

Farewell,
        dispensor of favors,
            guide,
                giver of good things.

THE HYMN TO ARES

Ares, superior force,
Ares, chariot rider,
Ares wears gold helmet,
Ares has mighty heart,
Ares, shield-bearer,
Ares, guardian of city,
Ares has armor of bronze,
Ares has powerful arms,
Ares never gets tired,
Ares, hard with spear,
Ares, rampart of Olympos,
Ares, father of Victory
who herself delights in war,
Ares, helper of Justice,
Ares overcomes other side,
Ares, leader of most just men,
Ares carries staff of manhood,
Ares turns his fiery bright cycle
among the Seven-signed tracks
of the aether, where flaming chargers
bear him forever
over the third orbit!
Hear me,
helper of mankind,
dispensor of youth's sweet courage,
beam down from up there
your gentle light
on our lives,
and your martial power,
so that I can shake off
cruel cowardice
from my head,
and diminish that deceptive rush
of my spirit, and restrain

that shrill voice in my heart
that provokes me
to enter the chilling din of battle.
You, happy god,
give me courage,
let me linger
in the safe laws of peace,
and thus escape
from battles with enemies
and the fate of a violent death.

THE HYMN TO HERAKLES

It's Herakles,
                the son of Zeus,
      that I will sing now,
the greatest man that ever lived on earth!

Alcmene gave him birth
          in Thebes
                  with its beautiful places
after she made love
          to that black cloud,
              Zeus.
At first he wandered
          over earth and the inexpressible sea,
              and suffered.
He struggled hard,
          and he did many fantastic things,
              really extraordinary tasks!
Now on the other hand
          he lives on the beautiful top
              of snowy Olympos,
and he loves it;
          he lives with Hebe
              who has such pretty feet.
Hail, lord—
          son of Zeus:
                  grant us excellence,
                  give us wealth.

THE HYMN TO ASCLEPIOS

Now I begin
    a song about the Doctor
        Asclepios,
        healer of sicknesses,
        a son of Apollo—
            the divine Coronis bore him
            in the plain of Dotion
                (she,
                    the daughter of King Phlegyes)
    a great source of joy to mankind:
            he can charm away
            awful pains.

And so, sir:
    farewell.
                I am praying to you
                      with this song.

THE HYMN TO PAN

Tell me about that dear son of Hermes,
     Muse,
  with the goat-feet,
    and the two horns,
  the one who loves noise,
      who goes around
          in meadows
    with dancing nymphs
      that tramp even on
         rocky peaks
      that goats can't reach
        calling for

Pan,
   the pastoral god
     with magnificent hair,
        unwashed,
  who's got
    all the snow crests
       and mountain ridges
        and all the rocky roads

He goes about
  here and there
    in the thick shrubbcry
and sometimes
    he is drawn down to
      gentle streams
and sometimes
    he just wanders about
       on steep rocks
climbing up
   to the highest peak
     to watch his sheep

and often
    he runs across
        a great white mountain range
and often
    he comes down
        the side of mountains
killing animals.
    He has a very sharp eye.

And sometimes—
    but only in the evening—
        relaxing from the hunt,
    he makes music,
        playing a song
            on his flute—
                it's sweet
and no bird
        weeping a lament,
no bird crying
        the song of its honeyed voice
    in the leaves
        of Spring's many flowers
            could outrun him,
                Pan,
                    in song

And the mountain nymphs
    with clear voices
        go along with him,
            their feet excited,
    they sing too,
        by the springs of dark water—
        Echo wailing
            on the mountain-top

And the god
        on this side
    on that side

                    of the chorus
                            enters the dance
                    speeding his feet
                            into their midst, dancing
        the red skin of a lynx
                    on his back
                            for covering,
                his head delights in
                    the piercing songs
        in a soft meadow
                    where crocus and hyacinth
                    with their sweet fragrance
                    mix in with the grass
                            any-old-where

They sing about
            the blessed gods and great Olympos—

                    for example,
                    they sing about Hermes
                            the helper,
                            above all others,
                                how he is a quick messenger
                                for all the gods,
                        how he came to Arcadia
                            with its many springs,
                                the mother of sheep,
                        where his precinct,
                            Cyllene, is
                            And there,
                    though he was a god,
                            he had tended sheep,
                                with their rough fleece,
                            for a mortal man,
                    because he,
                            Hermes,
                    felt a sensual wave
                            coming over him

                            69

to make love with
               a nymph with beautiful hair,
                  the daughter of Dryops

                  It ended
          in happy marriage,
             and, in their rooms,
                she produced for Hermes
                   a dear son—
                        fantastic to look at,
                with goat-feet,
                      and two horns,
                         very noisy
                             but laughing
                                  sweetly
          Its mother
             jumped up and fled—
          instead of nursing it
                   she abandoned the child—
          she was scared
             as she looked at
                   its brutal face!
                   its heavy beard!

But Hermes,
          the helper,
          was overjoyed
             in his mind
          and he took it in his hands
             and received it.

And he hid the boy
   in the thick skin
      of a mountain rabbit
and he went immediately
   to the home
      of the immortal gods.
He set him down

next to Zeus
and the other immortal gods
and he showed them
his boy.
And all the immortal gods
were delighted
in their hearts
and more than anyone else even
Dionysos,
Bacchos

And they decided to call him
Pan
because he had delighted the minds of
all.

And so, lord,
I greet you,
and with this song
I would please you.
I will remember you
in my other songs.

THE HYMN TO APHRODITE

Ah Muse,
tell me about the things that Aphrodite
does, the golden one, the Cyprian one,
she who awakens a pleasant yearning in
gods, she who subdues the race of mortal
men, and the birds of Zeus, and all the
many animals that the land nourishes,
and the sea nourishes. The works of
the beautifully crowned Cytherean are
the concern of all of these.

But there are three minds that she is
unable to persuade, unable, that is,
to seduce: there is the daughter of Zeus
who carries the aegis, Athena with her
gleaming eyes. She doesn't like the things
that Aphrodite does, the things that the
golden one does. Wars are what she likes,
and the work of Ares: fights and battles
are what she likes. And she concerns herself
with the decorative arts: she was the first
to teach the workingmen of earth how to
make great chariots, and how to make their chariots
inwrought with bronze. And she's the one who
teaches soft-skinned young ladies the
decorative arts, she puts it in the mind of
each one.

The second one
that Aphrodite, lover of laughter, cannot
subdue in love is noisy Artemis with her
golden arrows. She likes her bow, and she
likes murdering animals on mountains.
She likes lyres and dances, women's thrilling
screams and shady woods, and she likes the

cities of just men.

And third,
the things that Aphrodite does are not
pleasing to that venerable virgin, Hestia,
whom Cronos in his craftiness first gave
birth to (and also last—thanks to Zeus
who carries the aegis), the lady that
Poseidon and Apollo were both after. She
didn't want them, she refused them firmly.
And she swore a great oath on it, one that
was fulfilled, touching the head of father
Zeus who carries the aegis, that she would
be a virgin every day, a divine goddess.
And father Zeus gave her a beautiful
privilege instead of a wedding-gift: he has
her sit in the center of the house to receive
the best in offerings. In all the temples
of the gods she is honored, and among all
mortals she is a venerated goddess.

These are the three
minds that she is unable to persuade, that
is, to seduce. But nobody else, none of the
blessed gods, no mortal man, no one else can
ever escape Aphrodite. She even leads astray
the mind of Zeus himself, the lover of lightning,
the greatest of all, the one who receives the
greatest honor. And when she wants to, she
can deceive that sage heart of his easily,
and make even him mate with mortal women,
hiding from Hera, his sister and wife, she
who maintains the finest beauty among the
immortal goddesses, she whom Cronos in his
craftiness and mother Rheia bore to be
glorious, she whom Zeus, with his endless
concerns, has made his respected and trusted
wife.

                    But Zeus
put in Aphrodite's heart in turn a pleasant
yearning to mate with a mortal man, so that,
immediately, she would not be able to resist
a mortal man's bed, and boast some day to
all the gods that she, Aphrodite, lover of
laughter, with a sweet smile had mated the
gods with mortal women and they bore mortal
sons to immortal gods, and that she mated
goddesses with mortal men.

                    And it was for Anchises
therefore that he put in her heart a
pleasant longing, who at the time was
grazing his cattle on the mountain heights
of Ida, with its many springs, his body
very much like a god. And when she saw
him, Aphrodite, lover of laughter, she
loved him, and a terrifying desire seized
her heart.

                    She went away
to Cyprus, and entered her fragrant
temple at Paphos, where she has a precinct
and a fragrant altar. After going inside
she closed the bright doors, and the
Graces gave her a bath, they oiled her
with sacred olive-oil, the kind that the
gods always have on, that pleasant ambrosia
that she was perfumed with. Having put on
all her beautiful
clothing, and having ornamented herself
in gold, Aphrodite, lover of laughter,
hurried away to Troy, leaving sweet-smelling
Cyprus, quickly cutting a path through
the clouds high up.

                    And she came to Ida

with its many springs, the mother of
animals. She went right up the mountain
to the sheepfolds. Behind her moved grey
wolves, fawning on her, and bright-eyed
lions, bears, and quick, insatiable panthers.
When she saw them she felt joy in her
heart, and she put longing in their breasts,
and immediately they all went into the
shade of the valley in twos to sleep
with each other.

                    She herself
went to the huts, which were well-made.
She found him in the huts, left
all alone, alone from all the others,
the hero Anchises, who had beauty from
the gods. The others had followed their
cattle into the grasslands, all of them,
except him, he was in the huts,
left all alone, alone from all the others,
walking around here and there, playing on
his lyre thrillingly.

             She stood in front of him—
Aphrodite, the daughter of Zeus—in the
form and size of a young virgin, lest
he recognize her, lest he be frightened
in his eyes. Anchises saw her and he
marvelled at her, he was astonished by
her form, and size, and by her expensive
clothes. She wore a robe that was brighter
than a fire-flash, and she had on spiral
ringlets, and bright ornaments,
and necklaces around her delicate neck
that were very beautiful, and lovely, and
golden, and finely wrought, shining like
the moon on her delicate breasts, and
astonishing. Love gripped Anchises, and he

75

spoke these words to her:

          "Hello, great lady,
you must be one of the gods coming to visit
my house here, Artemis or Leto or the golden
Aphrodite or noble Themis or bright-eyes Athena—
or you're one of the Graces coming to visit me
here, who hang around with the gods and are called
immortal—or you're one of the nymphs who live
in beautiful groves—
or you're one of the nymphs who live on
this beautiful mountain here, the source
of rivers and grassy meadows. I'll build
an altar to you, on some high spot that
can be seen from all around, I'll offer
beautiful sacrifices to you in every season.
And in the goodness of your heart, make me
into a magnificent man among the Trojans!
Make my descendants flourish later on!
Let me live well for a long time, seeing
the light of the sun, rich among my people!
Let me attain the threshold of old age!"

          And Aphrodite,
the daughter of Zeus, replied to him:
"Anchises, the most splendid man who lives
on the earth, I'm not at all a goddess.
Why do you take me for one of the immortals?
On the contrary, I'm a mortal, and the mother
who bore me was just a woman. My father's
famous name is Otreus—perhaps you've heard
of him—he rules over all of Phrygia with
its great walls. And I know your language as well
as I know my own. The nurse who brought me up
in our palace was Trojan. She took care of me
from the moment I was a tiny child, right out of
the arms of my dear mother. That's why I know
your language as well as I know my own.

76

Argeiphontes with his golden wand has just
snatched me from the dances of noisy Artemis
with her golden arrows. We were playing,
many of us nymphs and well-endowed virgins,
and a huge crowd started to circle around us.
That's when Hermes with his golden wand
snatched me away. He brought me over
many lands ploughed by mortal men, many that
belonged to nobody, many that were untouched,
where man-eating animals roam in shaded
valleys. It seemed that my feet would never touch
earth again, the source of life.

                  He told me
that in the bed of Anchises I would be called
a lawful wife, and that I would bear you
splendid babies. And when he had pointed this
out, and told me, the powerful Hermes went back
to the race of immortals. But I've come to you,
and strong was the force that brought me.
I beg you, in the name of Zeus and your noble
parents—for surely no bad people could have
produced such a person as you—take me,
virgin that I am, ignorant of love-making
as I am, and present me to your father
and your good mother and to your brothers,
born from the same stock as you. I won't be
a daughter-in-law unfitting for them, but very fitting.
Send a messenger immediately to the Phrygians
with their fast horses to tell my father
and my worried mother. And they'll send back
gold and plenty of woven garments, and you,
you receive these splendid things as a dowry.
And after you've done these things, prepare a
pleasant wedding-feast, so liked by mortal men
and by the immortal gods."
                  Saying this,
the goddess filled his heart with a sweet

longing. And love seized Anchises, and he spoke
these words:

             "If you really are
a mortal, and the mother that bore you
really was a woman, and if Otreus is in fact
the famous name of your father, as you say,
and if you do really come here through the will
of the immortal guide, Hermes, then you will be
called my wife for all time. No one, no god,
no mortal man will stop me right here and now
from making love to you immediately. Even if
the great Archer Apollo himself should fire groaning
arrows from his silver bow—why I would even
consent to disappear into the house of Hades
after mounting your bed, lady, you who look
so much like a goddess."
                    And saying this
he took her hand. Aphrodite, smiling, turned
her head and advanced, with her beautiful eyes lowered,
toward his bed, which was well laid-out, and where
soft garments were strewn about for the prince.
Upon it were the skins of bears and roaring
lions, which he had himself killed in the high
mountains. When they had climbed into the bed that
was so well-made, he first of all took off the bright
ornaments from her body, brooches and spiral ringlets
and flower-like necklaces. He took off her beautiful
clothes and removed her girdle and put them on a
silver chair, he, Anchises! And then, by the will
and fate of the gods, he slept, a mortal, with an
immortal goddess. And he didn't even know it.

            At that moment,
when shepherds turn back their cattle to the stable,
and their sturdy sheep from flowering meadows,
at that moment she put a deep and pleasant sleep
over Anchises, and then she dressed herself

in her beautiful clothes. And after she put on
all her things, the divine goddess then stood up
in the tent, and her head touched its well-made
top, and from her cheeks shone an ambrosial beauty,
just as it is on the crowned Cytherean. She woke him
from his sleep and she spoke a word with him:

"Get up,
son of Dardanus! Why do you sleep such a deep sleep?
And tell me if I appear to you now to be the same
as when you first saw me with your eyes?"

So she spoke.
He did what she said and came out of his sleep
very rapidly. But when he saw her neck and the
beautiful eyes of Aphrodite, he was scared, and
he turned his eyes away to the side. Then he
covered his own beautiful face with his cloak,
and begging her, he spoke these words:

"Right then
when I first saw you with my eyes, goddess,
I knew you were divine. But you didn't speak honestly
to me. Now at your knees I implore you, in the name of
Zeus who carries the aegis, don't permit me to live
impotent among men from now on. Pity me. For a man
who sleeps with immortal goddesses loses his
potency."

Aphrodite,
the daughter of Zeus, then replied:

"Anchises,
most glorious of mortal men, cheer up!
Don't scare yourself out of your senses
so much! You have nothing terrible to fear
from me, nor from the other gods, because
the gods love you. You will have a fine son,

who will rule among the Trojans, and children
will be born forever to his children.
And his name shall be called Aeneas,
because the anguish that has come to me
is so terrible, since I let myself sleep
with a mortal man. And those mortal men
who in beauty and form come nearest
to the gods will always be from your stock.
It was for his beauty that wise Zeus
grabbed the blond Ganymede, so that
he might live among the gods and serve them
wine in the house of Zeus. He's a wonder
to behold, and honored by all the gods
as he pours red nectar out of a golden bowl.
And a pitiless grief seized the mind of Tros,
not knowing where the divine storm had snatched
away his dear son. And he mourned for him
every single day. And Zeus pitied him,
and gave him as payment for his son
the same fast-footed horses that carry
the gods! He gave them to him as a gift!
And Hermes the guide, by order of Zeus,
told him all the details, that he would be
immortal, and like the gods, never
get old. And when he heard the message of Zeus,
he didn't mourn anymore, he rejoiced
in his heart! He was delighted to go around
with horses as fast as storms!
And there was another man of your race,
Tithonus, who was like the gods, and whom Dawn,
golden-throned, snatched away. And she went
begging to Zeus in his dark clouds that he
make him immortal and that he live for all time.
And Zeus nodded to her and fulfilled her wish.
How foolish! She didn't know enough,
that lady, Dawn, to use her head and ask for youth,
ask to have old age rubbed away. Well,
as long as he possessed his very attractive youth,

he enjoyed playing with golden-throned Dawn,
daughter of morning, and he lived on the shores
of Ocean, at the ends of the earth.
But when the first grey hairs came out
on his beautiful head and in his noble beard,
then the lady Dawn got out of his bed.
She took him into her house and nourished him,
with food and ambrosia, and she gave him
beautiful clothes. But when hateful old age
had completely hit him, and he wasn't able to
move his limbs or even lift them, then it was
that this idea seemed best to her: she simply
put him in a room and closed the bright doors.
His voice flows on endlessly, but there isn't
any of that old kick left in his gnarled bones.
And I wouldn't want you to be among the immortals
like that, and be immortal, and live forever.
But if you were to live as you are now,
with your present form and body, and if you
were to be called my husband, then no grief would
ever overcome my sturdy spirit. But in fact
a cruel old age will soon overtake you, the
heartless kind that comes to men, killing,
wearisome, the kind that even the gods hate.
As for me, there will be great disgrace for me
among the immortal gods every single day continuously
because of you. Before this they feared my words
and my plans, since I mated all the immortal gods
with mortal women. For my mind ruled over all of them.
Now on the other hand I don't dare even open my mouth
on this subject with the immortals, since I was
very much infatuated, miserably, unmentionably.
I was knocked out of my mind, and I'm carrying a child
in my womb, having slept with a mortal. And, when he
will see the light of day, the big-breasted mountain
nymphs will care for him, those who live on this great
sacred mountain. They are not quite mortals and not quite
immortals. They live a long time, and eat divine foods,
and do dances beautifully with the immortals. It's with

them that the Silenuses and sharp-eyed Hermes make love
in the corner of their charming caves. At the same time
as their birth, there are trees, pines and high oaks,
that grow up on the earth that nourishes man, and they're
beautiful, flourishing on these high mountains. They
stand very tall, and their grove is called a sacred precinct
of the immortals. Men never cut these with an axe. But
when their moment for death is upon them, they simply
dry up in the ground these pretty trees, and their bark
withers away, and their branches fall to the ground.
At the same time, the spirit of the nymphs leaves the light
of the sun. And it's these who will take my son and bring
him up among them. But I, so that I may go through all the things
I have in mind, I shall come back in the fifth year and bring
you our son. And then when you see the child for the first
time with your own eyes you will be delighted with what you
see. He'll look very much like a god. And you can take him
around then to the windy city of Troy.
And if any mortal man ever asks you
who the mother was that carried this sweet boy
in her womb, remember to give him this story,
as I order you to: "They say he's the child
of a flower-like nymph, one of those who live
on this mountain covered with woods."
But if you ever tell, and go boasting
with a foolish head that you made love with
the crowned Cytherean, Zeus will be furious
and strike you with a smoky thunderbolt.
And now you've heard everything.
Guard this secret in your own head
and don't mention my name: avoid the wrath
of the gods."

          She said this,
and then shot up into the windy sky.
          Farewell, goddess,
you who rule over Cyprus with its great buildings.
Now that I have begun with a hymn for you,
I will pass on to another theme.

THE SECOND HYMN TO APHRODITE

Venerable,
               golden-crowned,
   beautiful Aphrodite
   is who I shall sing,
she who has
   all the high locations of Cyprus,
      the sea place,
         where the damp force
            of Zephyros breathing
               carried her along
                  on waves
                     of the resounding sea
                        in soft foam.
In their own fillets of gold
   the Hours
      received her
      happily
and happily
   put the ambrosial garments
      around her.
On her immortal head
   they placed a crown
      that was carefully made,
         beautiful and in gold,
and in the pierced lobes of her ears
   they placed
   flowers of copper
      and precious gold.
On her delicate neck
   and her silver-white breasts
      they arranged
      necklaces of gold,
   which they have themselves made,
      which the Hours, themselves,
         in their own fillets of gold,

wear when they go
        to the pleasant dance
        of the gods
    in the house of their father.

And then,
    when they had placed
    all this decoration
        on her body,
        they led her
        to the immortals.
And they welcomed her
    when they saw her
    and they reached out their hands
                to her
    and each one of them
                yearned
        to make her
            his legal wife
    and to take her home,
        as they all
            gawked
        at the figure
            of the Cytherean
    crowned in violets.

Farewell,
        quick-blinking,
                sweet-smiling,
        grant me the victory
            in this contest:
        favor my song
        and I will remember you
        in another song.

THE THIRD HYMN TO APHRODITE

The Cytherean
    born at Cyprus
        is who I shall sing,
she who presents
    humans
        with such nice presents.
That seductive face of hers
    is always smiling, always
        carrying its seductive flower.
Hello, goddess,
    sovereign of Salamis
        with its good buildings,
            and of the sea place, Cyprus.
Give me the kind of song
    that seduces, please,
        and I will remember you
            in another one.

THE HYMN TO HEPHAISTOS

The skill
of Hephaistos
is famous
do sing it
clear
Muse
he taught men
work
with bright-eyes
Athena
work that was
noble
for men to do
on the earth
men who
formerly
lived in
caves
in mountains
like animals
now on the
other hand
thanks to
Hephaistos
whose skill is
so famous
they know
how to
work
life is
easy
the whole
year
long
and they live it

quietly
in their
houses now
but be
gracious
Hephaistos
do give us
excellence
please
give us
wealth

THE HYMN TO POSEIDON

It's about Poseidon
that great god
that I'm going to begin
singing
the mover of earth
and the empty sea
the great water
god
who owns Helicon
and that big town
Aegae earth-
shaker
whom the gods gave
double honors
you are
controller
of horses
saviour of ships
hello Poseidon
earth-
carrier dark-
haired and happy
god your heart is
good
help sailors

THE HYMN TO ZEUS

Zeus
who is the best
god
and the greatest
is who
I will sing
he sees
far he rules
he
finishes things
he converses
wisely
with Themis
at his side
be kind
son of
Cronus
who sees far
you're the most
famous
of all
you're the greatest

THE HYMN TO THE MUSES

I begin
with the Muses
and with Apollo
and Zeus
because
it's through
the Muses
and the archer
Apollo
that there are men
on earth
singers and
lyre players
and because
it's through Zeus
there are kings

you're a lucky man
if the Muses
like you
sweet
is the sound
that flows
from your mouth
hail
children
of Zeus
favor
my song

I
will remember
you
in another

THE HYMN TO DEMETER

And now let me sing
Demeter,
that awesome goddess,
with her beautiful hair,
her
and her daughter
with slender feet,
whom Aidoneus
carried away,
and Zeus,
who sees far,
in his deep voice,
allowing it,
far away from
Demeter
and her gold sword,
her good harvests,
to play
with those big-breasted
daughters of Oceanos,
picking flowers,
roses
and crocus
and beautiful violets,
in lush meadow,
and iris,
and hyacinth,
narcissus even
which Earth,
as a trick,
grew
for this girl,
as a favor for
Him Who Receives So Many,
and with Zeus

allowing it
(its brightness
was wonderful!).
It astonished everyone
who saw it,
immortal gods
and mortal men
alike.
From its root
it pushed up
a hundred heads
and a fragrance
from its top
making
all the vast sky above
smile,
and all the earth,
and all the salt swelling
of the sea.
And she
was astonished too,
she stretched out
both her hands
to pick
this delightful thing.
But the earth,
wide with roads,
opened up!
in the Nysian Plain,
and out came
He Who Receives So Many,
with his immortal horses,
that son of Cronos
with so many names.
And he grabbed her,
resisting,
and he took her
in his gold chariot,

weeping.
She screamed
in shrill voice
calling for
Zeus
her supreme and powerful
father.
But nobody,
no one of the immortals.
no one of mortal men,
heard her voice
anymore than
the olives
with their good harvests
heard her voice—
except Hecate,
daughter of Persaeus
in her bright headband,
alone in her tenderness,
who heard her
from her cave,
and our lord the Sun,
splendid son of Hyperion,
he too heard the girl
calling her father,
Zeus.
But Zeus
was sitting far away
from the gods
in a temple
where many suppliants came,
where he received
many beautiful offerings
from mortal men.
And so,
though she resisted,
he drove on
(for Zeus had planned it)

with his immortal horses,
the brother of her father,
The Ruler of Many,
He Who Receives So Many,
that son of Cronos
with so many names.
And as long as
the goddess
could see the earth
and the star sky
and the sea with its fish
churning,
and as long as
she could hope to see
her mother again,
and the race of gods
who are forever,
that hope
charmed her great heart,
though grieving . . . .
And the mountain peaks
echoed
with her immortal voice,
and the depths of the sea,
and her noble mother
heard her.
A sharp pain
seized her heart.
With her lovely hands
she tore the headdress
on her immortal hair,
she threw off
the dark covering
on her shoulders,
and she shot out,
like a bird,
over dry land
and sea,

searching.
But nobody,
neither of gods
nor of mortal men,
nobody
wanted to tell her
the truth,
not even
one of the birds,
who bring such
messages of truth,
came to her.
And then,
for nine days,
the noble Deo
turned about the earth,
holding in her hands
torch light
and not once did she taste
ambrosia,
or that sweet brew,
nectar,
for she was grieving.
Nor did she once
plunge her body
in bath.
But when dawn ten
appeared,
luminous,
Hecate
encountered her,
holding a light
in her hands,
and bringing her news,
she spoke to her,
she said:
"Demeter,
bringer of seasons,

with your great gifts,
who
of the heavenly gods
or of mortal men
carried away
Persephone
and grieved
your good heart?
I heard a voice
but I didn't see
with my eyes
who it was.
I tell you
the whole truth,
it's that short."
So spoke Hecate.
And the daughter
of Rheia,
with her beautiful hair,
said nothing
in reply,
she shot away,
very fast,
with her,
carrying the light
in her hands.
They went
to the Sun,
that observer
of gods and men,
they stood
in front of his horses
and the sacred goddess asked:
"Sun,
treat me with honor,
if ever
I have pleased your heart
with what I say

or what I do.
The girl
that I bore,
that flower,
glorious
in her beauty—
I've heard
her lovely voice
in this empty air
as if she were being
overpowered,
but I didn't see her
with my eyes.
But you,
you look down
with your rays
from the divine air
on all the earth
and sea,
tell me
honestly
if you've seen
anyone getting away,
taking her,
unwilling,
away from me,
by force,
my dear child,
some god or
some mortal man."
She spoke.
And the son of Hyperion
answered her:
"Demeter,
daughter of Rheia
with her beautiful hair,
you shall now know.
I respect

and pity you
greatly,
grieving
for your daughter
with her slender feet.
There is no other god
responsible
but Zeus,
who gathers the clouds,
who gave her
to Hades,
his own brother,
to be called
his wife.
He took her,
carrying her off
on his horses,
profusely screaming,
down
into mist darkness.
But goddess,
stop
your own great weeping.
It does not fit you,
this anger that's
so vain
and insatiate.
He is not unworthy
as son-in-law
among the gods,
Aidoneus,
The Ruler of Many,
your own brother,
your own blood.
For honors,
he obtained his lot
when originally
the division in three

took place.
He lives now
with those over whom
he was allotted
to be king."
He said this
and called his horses,
and they,
at the sound of his voice,
immediately
brought his chariot,
like long-winged birds.
Yet sharper pain,
more savage even,
struck her heart:
outraged with Zeus
wrapped in his clouds,
she withdrew
from the company of gods
and from great Olympos,
she went to
the cities of men
and their grasslands,
disguising her beauty
for a long time.
And no one
who saw her
recognized her,
no man,
no deep-girdled
woman,
no one
until she reached the house
of prudent Celeus,
who was ruler
of the fragrant town
of Eleusis.
Her heart

saddened,
she sat down
near the road,
at the Virgin's Well,
where the citizens come
to draw water.
She sat
in the shade
(overhead
there grew
a tuft of olives)
looking like
an old woman
who was beyond
child-bearing,
beyond the gifts
of Aphrodite,
the lover of garlands—
like the nurses of
the children of kings
who administer law
or like their servants
in those echoing
houses.
The daughters of Celeus,
son of Eleusis
saw her,
as they came
for the easy task
of drawing water
in their bronze pails
to take home
to their father,
the four of them,
like goddesses,
in the flower of youth,
Callidice
and Cleisidice,

and lovely Demo,
and Callithoe,
the oldest of all.
They didn't recognize her.
It's hard
for gods to be recognized
by mortals.
They stood by her,
they spoke to her:
"Where are you from,
old woman,
you who are from
another age?
Why
have you bypassed
the city,
why
didn't you approach
the houses?
There are women there,
in the shady halls,
your age,
and younger ones
who would befriend you
with what they say
and what they do."
They spoke,
and the goddess
replied
"Hello,
good children
of the feminine sex,
whoever you are.
I am going to tell you
something.
It is not improper
to tell you the truth,
in reply to your questions.

My name is
Doso.
That's the name
my mother gave me.
I just came here
from Crete,
over the wide back
of the sea,
against my will,
for pirates took me
against my will
with force and violence.
They went
in their swift ship
to Thoricos,
where hordes of women
got off
onto the land,
and the men too,
and they held a feast
by the stern of the ship,
but my heart wanted no food,
and secretly
I ran away
onto that dark land
and I fled
those arrogant masters,
to cheat them
of the prize
of selling me,
not having bought me
in the first place.
So I've come here
in my wandering,
and I don't even know
what land this is,
or who
its inhabitants are.

But may the gods
who live on Olympos
grant you
young husbands,
and may they let you
bear the children
their parents want.
Be gracious
and pity me, girls.
Dear children,
whose house can I go to,
what man
or woman's
where I might work
graciously
for them,
the sort of work
that is proper for
an elderly woman?
Gladly
I would hold
a new-born child
in my arms
and nurse him,
and I would take care of
the house,
and make the beds
in the master's sturdy rooms,
and oversee the women's work."
The goddess spoke.
And Callidice,
the most beautiful
of the daughters of Celeus,
a virgin, unmarried,
replied:
"Mother,
we who are human
have to endure

103

gifts from the gods,
though hard,
for they are stronger
than we are
by far.
These things
I shall counsel you in
exactly,
and I shall name for you
those men
who have great power
and honor here,
those who are the foremost
of our people,
who defend the walls
of our city
with their will
and their straight laws.
There's the very wise
Triptolemos,
and Diocles,
and Polyxeinus,
the irreproachable Eumolpos,
and Dolichos,
and our own valiant father—
of whom
all have wives
to take care of the house.
But no one of them,
after one glance,
could mistake
your beauty,
and chase you away
from the house.
No,
they would welcome you.
You look like
a god.

If you want to,
wait here
until we get to our father's house
and tell our mother,
Metanira,
all about this,
to see if she'll not
beg you to come
to our place,
rather than
have you look elsewhere.
There is a son
growing up
in our sturdy palace,
who was born
late,
long desired
and much loved.
If you
were to take care of him
up to his youth,
you would be envied
easily
by those of the female sex
who see you,
for the wages you would get
for your nursing
would be so much!"
So she spoke.
And the goddess
nodded her head.
They filled their shining pails
with water
and they carried them away
rejoicing.
Quickly
they reached
the great house

of their father,
and immediately
they told their mother
what they saw and
what they heard.
And she
ordered them
to run very fast
and summon her,
for a large salary.
And like deer,
like calves
in the season of
Spring
who leap
in the meadow
when they're glutted
with food,
they ran out
on the hollow road,
lifting first
the folds of their lovely gowns
and around their shoulders
their hair,
like crocus bloom,
shot out.
They came upon
the glorious goddess
near the road
where they left her before.
And then they led her
to the house
of their father,
she going behind them,
grieving
her good heart,
and veiled
from the head down,

a dark garment
twisting around
the delicate feet
of the goddess.
Quickly
they reached the house
of Celeus,
who was cherished by Zeus,
and they crossed
the portico,
where their mother sat
waiting for them
near the door posts
so solidly roofed,
holding in her lap
an infant,
a new flower.
And when they had run over to her,
the goddess
put her foot on the threshold
and touched her head
on the ceiling
and filled the doorway
with a divine light.
Awestruck,
and with respect,
fear
turned their mother pale!
She got up
from her couch
and bid the goddess
sit down.
But Demeter
who brings the seasons,
whose gifts are so brilliant,
did not want to sit down
on such a splendid couch,
but waited,

in silence,
her lovely eyes thrust downward,
until
the perceptive Iambe
brought her a chair,
over which she threw
a silver fleece.
Then the goddess sat down
and drew down her veil
with her hands.
And for a long time
she sat on this chair
grieving
and silent,
without embracing anyone
with a word
or an act.
Without smiling,
without eating
food
or drink,
she sat there,
wasting away with longing
for her daughter
in her low dress,
until
the perceptive Iambe,
with jokes
and with much clowning around
forced
this sacred lady
to smile,
to laugh,
and to
cheer up her spirits.
It was she too
who later pleased her
in angry moments.

And Metanira
filled a cup with wine,
sweet like honey,
and gave it to her,
but she refused,
because,
she said,
it was unlawful for her
to drink red wine,
and instead,
she asked her
to mix some water
with barley
and tender pennyroyal,
to be given that
to drink.
And she prepared
the mixture
and gave it to the goddess
as ordered.
And the very noble
Deo
took it
for the rite.
And Metanira
in her beautiful dress
began to talk to her:
"Hail, woman,
I gather
you were not born
of common parents
but of good ones,
for in your eyes
there shows
a majesty,
a grace
as if of kings
who administer law.

109

But we who are human
have to endure
gifts from the gods,
though hard.
For a yoke
lies on our necks.
But now that you've come here,
everything I have
is at your disposal.
Take care of
this child
whom the gods brought us,
born very late
and unexpected,
and whom I prayed for
very much.
If you
take care of him,
up to his youth,
you will be envied
by those of the female sex
who see you,
for the wages I will pay
for your nursing
will be so much!"
Demeter
with her beautiful hair,
answered her:
"And hail to you in turn,
woman,
and may the gods bring you
good things.
I gladly accept
the care of your son
as you ask me.
I will nurse him
and I do not think
he will suffer

from any carelessness
on the part of his nurse,
or from any bewitching
or any magic plants.
And I know
a strong antidote
for teething.
I know
a good precaution against
the perils of witchcraft."
And as she said this
she took him
with her immortal hands
to her fragrant breast.
His mother
was delighted.
So she brought up
in the palace
Demophoön,
prudent Celeus'
splendid son,
whose mother was
Metanira
in her beautiful dress.
And he grew up
like a god,
without feeding
from her breast,
without any food at all!
Demeter
anointed him
with ambrosia,
as if
he were born from a god,
she breathed on him
sweetly
as she held him
in her lap.

111

At night
she held him
in a powerful fire,
like a torch,
in secret
from his good parents.
And it was a matter
of great astonishment
to them
to see him growing up
ahead of his time,
and with an appearance
like gods.
And the goddess
would have made him
ageless,
deathless even,
were it not for
the rashness of
Metanira
in her beautiful dress
one night,
who, spying,
saw this
from her fragrant bedroom.
She screamed
and she beat her thighs,
frightened
for her child,
and completely
outraged
in her heart,
and she spoke
these words,
wailing:
"Baby Demophoön,
the stranger
hides you in all that fire

and makes me weep
and brings me bitter pain."
She spoke,
wailing.
And the goddess
heard her.
Demeter,
with her beautiful hair,
was furious with her,
and with her immortal hands
she lifted the child
out of the fire,
this child
whose mother bore it
in the palace long after
a child had ceased to be hoped for.
She picked it up
and threw it
on the ground,
her heart was terribly
enraged,
and at the same time
she said this
to Metanira
in her beautiful dress:
"Stupid people,
brainless,
you don't even know
when fate
is bringing you something good,
or something bad.
And now,
by your stupidity,
you've done yourself
the worst possible harm.
I swear
a divine oath,
by the waters of Styx,

which are implacable:
I would have made
your dear child
deathless,
ageless—
forever!
I would have done him
an undying honor.
But now it's impossible
for him to escape
the fate of death.
Yet he will always have
at least this
undying honor,
because of the fact that
he climbed on my knees,
and slept in my arms.
When he comes to his prime
with the passing years,
the sons of Eleusis
will make war
and terrible battles
with each other
every day
forever.
I am the honorable
Demeter,
producer of
the greatest blessing,
the greatest joy,
for man
and god
alike.
But come now,
have all the people
build for me
a huge temple
and an altar

beneath it,
below the acropolis
and its high wall,
above the Callichoros,
on the protruding hill.
And I myself
will inaugurate
the mysteries,
so that
in doing them
piously
you will please
my heart."
The goddess
said this
and changed
her size
and shape,
throwing away
her agedness,
and beauty
drifted
all around her
and a lovely fragrance
from her perfumed veils
spread about
and a brightness
from the immortal flesh
of the goddess
shone far away
and her blond hair
fell
to her shoulders
and the sturdy house
was filled with light
like lightning.
She walked
around the rooms,

while Metanira
felt her knees buckling,
after being speechless
for a long time,
not even remembering
to pick up
her very special child
from the ground.
But his sisters
heard
his pitiful voice,
and they jumped up
from their plush
couches.
One of them
took the child
in her arms
and held it
to her breast.
Another one
revived the fire.
Another one
ran
on her tender feet
to help take her mother
from this fragrant room.
And they all gathered around
the child,
who was gasping,
they washed him
and they babied him.
But its anger
could not be soothed!
For these were
inferior nurses
who held it now,
these nurses were
inferior.

They spent the whole night
trying to soothe
the noble goddess,
though they were shaking
with fear.
When dawn appeared
they gave an exact account
to Celeus
whose power goes far,
as the goddess
told them to,
Demeter
in her beautiful crown.
And he summoned
his boundless people
to assembly,
and ordered them
to build,
for Demeter
in her beautiful hair,
a sumptuous temple,
and an altar,
on the protruding hill.
And they heard his voice
and immediately
set to it.
They built
as he ordered.
And it grew
according to the will
of the goddess.
And when they were finished
and done with their work,
each one went home.
Then the blond Demeter
installed herself there,
far away from
all the happy gods,

she stayed there,
wasting away
with longing
for her daughter
in her low dress.
And she made this
the most terrible year
on this earth
that feeds so many,
and the most cruel.
The earth
did not take seed
that year,
for Demeter
in her beautiful crown
concealed it.
And the cattle
many times
pulled
their bent ploughs
in vain
over the land,
and many times
the white barley
fell
uselessly
upon the earth.
And in fact
she would have wiped out
the whole race
of talking men
with a painful famine,
and deprived
those who live on Olympos
of the glorious honor
of offerings and sacrifices,
if Zeus
hadn't noticed it,

and thought about it
in his heart.
First of all
he sent Iris
on her wings of gold
to call Demeter
in her beautiful hair,
whose beauty was
very great.
He told her
and she obeyed
Zeus
in his dark clouds
and ran
the whole distance
quickly
on her feet.
She reached
the city
of fragrant Eleusis
and found
Demeter
in the temple
veiled in black,
and she spoke to her
and said this:
"Demeter,
father Zeus
whose knowledge
is endless
calls upon you
to come back
among the race of gods
who are forever.
Come on,
don't let
the word of Zeus
go unfulfilled."

She spoke,
begging her.
But the heart of the goddess
was not convinced.
So
their father
then sent out
every one of the blessed gods,
who are forever,
one after another.
Each in turn
went
and summoned her,
and gave her
many very beautiful gifts
and honors,
those which she
would want to choose
among the gods.
But no one
was able to presuade
her mind and heart
because she was furious
inside,
and she rejected
their words
cold.
For she said
she would not ever again
set foot
on fragrant Olympos,
she would not
let the fruit of the earth
come up
until
she saw with her eyes
her daughter's
beautiful face.
And when Zeus

120

heard this,
in his deep voice,
and seeing far,
he dispatched
Argeiphontes
with his golden wand
to Erebos,
to exhort
Hades
with soft words
and to bring back
the gentle Persephone
from the dark mist
into the light again
among the gods,
so that
her mother,
seeing her
with her own eyes,
would abandon her anger.
Hermes
was not inattentive:
he left
the seat of Olympos
and plunged right down
into the depths of the earth.
And there
he met the king
inside his house
sitting on a couch
next to his venerable wife
who was very reluctant
because of a longing
for her mother.
But her mother was far off
and brooding on her terrible plan
because of the deeds of
the blessed gods.

121

The powerful Argeiphontes
stood
next to the god
and said:
"Hades,
in your dark hair,
king over the dead,
father Zeus
ordered me
to bring back
the beautiful Persephone
away from Erebos
and up with the gods,
so that her mother,
seeing her
with her own eyes,
would stop
her anger,
her terrible wrath
against the gods.
For she's thinking about
the enormous act
of wiping out
that weak race
of men
who are born on the earth,
concealing
their seeds
in the ground
and thus annihilating
the honors
of the gods.
She's got
a terrible anger,
and she doesn't mix
with the gods,
but she sits
far away from them

inside a fragrant temple,
and she never leaves
the rocky city
of Eleusis."
So he spoke.
King Aidoneus
of the underworld
smiled grimly
and did not disobey
the commands
of King Zeus.
Immediately
he told
the thoughtful Persephone:
"Go on,
Persephone,
back to your mother
in her black veil,
go with a kind heart.
Do not despair
too much:
it is useless.
As a husband
I will not be
unworthy of you
among the gods:
I am the brother
of your father,
Zeus.
When you're here,
you will reign
over everyone who lives
and moves,
and you will have
the greatest honors
among the gods.
And there will be
eternal punishment

for those who do wrong
and who do not
appease your heart
piously
with sacrifices
and great gifts."
So he spoke.
And the prudent Persephone
rejoiced
and jumped up
quickly
with joy.
But secretly
he slipped her
a pomegranate seed,
a sweet one,
to eat,
a precaution
so that
she would not stay
everyday
up there
with the venerable Demeter
in her black veil.
Aidoneus,
The Ruler of So Many,
hitched up
his immortal horses
in front of
their gold chariot.
She got up
in the chariot,
and the powerful Argeiphontes,
next to her,
took the reins
and the whip
in his good hands,
and sped

out through the palace.
The horses flew away
willingly.
They covered
the long route
quickly.
Neither the sea
nor the water of rivers,
nor the valleys of grass
nor the mountain tops
stopped
the force
of these immortal horses.
They cut the deep mist
over them
as they went.
Hermes,
who was driving,
stopped
in front of
the fragrant temple
where Demeter
in her beautiful crown
waited.
And when she saw them,
she leaped,
like a maenad
in the woods
on a shady mountain.
And Persephone,
from where she was . . .
her mother, descending . . .
she leaped down
to run . . .
and to her . . .
stopping . . .
"My child,
you should not have . . .

the food? tell me . . .
so that you could come up . . .
so that you might live
with me
and with your father,
Zeus
who gathers the clouds,
honored
by all the gods.
But if you go back
flying
into the depths
of the earth,
you will live there
for a third
of the seasons
of the year,
for the two other parts
you will live
with me
and the other gods.
And whenever
the earth
blossoms
with all kinds
of fragrant
Spring flowers,
you will come back up again
from the mist darkness,
to the great astonishment
of gods
and mortal men.
And with what trick
was it
that powerful
He Who Receives So Many
deceived you?"
The very beautiful Persephone

faced her
and said:
"Well, mother,
I will tell you everything
precisely.
When helpful Hermes,
that fast messenger,
came,
on behalf of Zeus
and the other gods,
to bring me out
of Erebos,
so that
you might see me
with your eyes
and cease your anger
with the gods
and your terrible wrath,
I immediately
jumped up for joy.
But secretly
he slipped me
a pomegranate seed
with a sweet taste,
and forced me,
unwillingly,
violently,
to eat it.
How he came
and seized me—
through a shrewd plan
of Zeus,
my father,
and carried me down
into the depths
of the earth,—
I will tell you,
and I will divulge

127

everything
that you ask.
We were all of us
in a lovely meadow,
Leucippe,
Phaino,
Electra and Ianthe,
and Melita
and Iache,
Rhodia and
Callirhoe,
Melobosis
and Tyche
and that beautiful flower,
Ocyrhoe,
Chryseis and
Ianira and
Ocaste and
Admeta and
Rhodope and
Plouto and
lovely Calypso,
and Styx and
Urania
and lovable Galaxaure
and Pallas
who moves you to battle,
and Artemis the archer,
we were playing
and cutting
lovely flowers
with our hands—
all mixed together:
tender crocus
and iris
and hyacinth,
rose-buds
and lilies that were

eye-catchers,
and narcissus
which the wide earth
grows like crocus.
And I was very happy
cutting them—
when the earth opened up
and out jumped
powerful King
He Who Receives So Many.
I put up
much resistance
but he took me
and went back down
under the earth
in his gold chariot.
I cried out
loud.
I tell you
all these things
truly,
though it grieves me."
They spent
the whole of that day
with hearts united,
and they warmed
each other's heart
with many gestures
of affection,
and her heart stopped
grieving.
They gave
and received
joy
from each other.
Then Hecate
came up to them,
in her bright headband,

and she showed
much affection for
the daughter of
sacred Demeter.
And from that day on
that lady
precedes and follows
Persephone.
And Zeus
whose voice is deep
and who sees far
sent a messenger
to them,
Rheia
with her beautiful hair,
to bring back
Demeter,
in her black veil,
to the race of gods.
He offered
to give her
whatever honors
she would choose
among the immortal gods.
He consented
that her daughter
would spend
a third part
of the year's cycle
in the mist darkness
and the two other parts
with her mother
and with the immortal gods.
He ordered this.
And the goddess
was not inattentive
to the message of Zeus.
Quickly

she leaped
down the peaks
of Olympos
and came
to Rarion,
what had been a fertile
and productive land
in the past,
but was now
no longer productive,
and fallow,
and leafless everywhere.
It concealed
the white barley,
according to the plan
of Demeter,
with her beautiful feet.
But it would soon boast
long ears of corn,
with Spring coming on.
and the fat furrows
of its soil
would be heavy with corn
tied in sheaves.
There the goddess first landed
out of the barren air,
and they were glad
to see each other,
and they rejoiced
in their hearts.
Then Rheia,
with her bright headband,
addressed her:
"Come here,
my child,
Zeus
with his deep voice
who sees far,

calls you to come up
with the race of gods,
and he offers to give you
whatever honors you want
among the gods.
He consents
that your daughter
would spend
a third part
of the year's cycle
in the mist darkness
and the two other parts
with you
and the other gods.
He consented
with a nod of his head.
But come,
my child,
and obey him,
and don't be too angry
with Zeus
in his dark clouds.
And make the crops
productive, now,
for humans."
She said this,
and Demeter,
in her beautiful crown,
was not inattentive.
Immediately
she brought in a harvest
from fertile lands.
And the whole earth
was weighted
with leaves and flowers.
And she went
and taught the kings
who administer law,

Triptolemos and
Diocles the horseman,
and mighty Eumolpos
and Celeus, the leader
of the people,
she taught them
the ministry of her rites,
and she revealed to them
her beautiful mysteries,
which are impossible
to transgress,
or to pry into,
or to divulge:
for so great
is one's awe
of the gods
that it stops
the tongue.
Happy
is that man,
among the men
on earth,
who witnesses
these things.
And whoever
is not initiated
in the rites,
whoever
has no part in them,
he does not share
the same fate,
when he dies
and is down in
the squalid darkness.
And when the divine goddess
had accomplished everything,
they went up
to Olympos

to join the company
of the other gods.
That's where they live,
these sacred
and venerable goddesses,
near to Zeus
who enjoys the lightning.
And very happy
is that man,
among the men
on earth,
whom they
graciously
decide to love.
Immediately
they send
Ploutos
to the man's great house,
to his hearth,
and he gives
wealth
to mortal men.
But come,
you who possess
the fragrant town
of Eleusis
and Paros
that is surrounded
by water,
and rocky Antron,
you, lady,
who bears
such great gifts,
who brings
the seasons,
sovereign,
Deo,

you and your
very beautiful daughter,
Persephone,
be kind, and,
in exchange for
my poem,
give me the kind of life
my heart wants.
I
will remember you
in my other poems.

THE SECOND HYMN TO DEMETER

I begin
by singing
Demeter
in her beautiful hair,
majestic,
goddess,
Demeter,
her and her
very beautiful daughter,
Persephone.

Greetings,
goddess!
Preserve
this city and
direct
this song.

THE HYMN TO ATHENA

I'll start this singing with
that grand goddess,
Pallas Athena,
bright-eyes,
so shrewd,
her heart inexorable,
as virgin, redoubtable,
protectress of cities,
powerful,
Tritogene,
whom shrewd Zeus himself
produced
out of his sacred head—
bedecked in that
spangly gold war armor
she wears—
what awe enthralled
all those immortals
who saw her
jump suddenly
out of his sacred head
shaking
her sharp spear,
right out of Zeus
who holds the aegis!
Great Olympos itself
shook terribly
under the might
of bright-eyes,
the earth groaned
awfully and the ocean
was moved to foam up
with dark waves,
then as sudden
the salt sea stopped.

The glorious son of Hyperion,
the sun, stood
his fast-footed horses still
for a long time,
until the girl
took that god-like armor
from her immortal shoulders.
Shrewd Zeus
laughed.

And so, greetings to you,
daughter of Zeus,
who holds the aegis.
I will remember you
in another song.

THE SECOND HYMN TO ATHENA

I'll start this singing with
that protectress of cities,
that terrible Pallas Athena,
who, with Ares,
takes care of
the work of war,
the destruction of cities
and the shouts of war,
she who watches out for
the army,
when it's coming and
when it's going.

Greetings, goddess!
Bring me good luck
and happiness.

THE HYMN TO HESTIA

Hestia,
you who have received the highest honor,
to have your seat forever
in the enormous houses of all the gods
and all the men who walk on the earth,
it is a beautiful gift you have received,
it is a beautiful honor.
Without you, mankind would have no feasts,
since no one could begin the first and last drink
of honey-like wine without an offering
to Hestia.

And you too, Argeiphontes, son of Zeus and Maia,
messenger of the gods with your gold wand,
giver of good things, be good to me,
protect me along with the venerable and dear
Hestia.
Come, both of you inhabit this beautiful house
with mutual feelings of friendship.
You accompany good work with intelligence
and youth.

Hello, daughter of Cronos,
you too, Hermes, with your gold wand.
As for me, I will remember you in another song.

THE SECOND HYMN TO HESTIA

Hestia,
you who take care of the holy house of Apollo
who shoots so far,
the house at sacred Pytho,
a liquid oil flows forever from your hair.
Come on into this house of mine,
come on in here with shrewd Zeus.
Be gracious towards my song.

THE HYMN TO THE SUN

Start now,
Muse Calliope,
     daughter of Zeus,
your singing of the Sun,
     blazing

                 and born of
                 She-Who-Shines-Far,
                     Euryphaëssa,
                 with her big eyes,
                 to the son of Earth
                 and the starred Sky

        Hyperion
        had married
            glorious Euryphaëssa,
           who was his own sister,
     and she made him beautiful children,
                Dawn
                who had rose arms,
                Moon
                who had lovely hair,
                Sun
                    who is tireless
                    and like the gods

He shines down on men
and immortal gods
as he rides in his chariot

Hard, he looks down
hard out of his golden helmet
       with his eyes

The bright rays beam out from him
       so brilliantly

The bright cheek-piece of his helmet
            around the temples of his head
            charmingly
encloses
the face that you can see from far away

A beautiful coat
            of fine workmanship
gleams on his body
            and blows
            in the wind
            over stallions that draw him

But then he stops
            the golden yoke
            of his chariot
                        and his horses
            and he drives them down again
                        across the sky
                                    into Ocean

Greetings, lord
Be kind,
            give me a life that is going to satisfy my heart

            And now,
            now that I started with you,
            I will celebrate
            the race of mortal men who are
                        half divine,
            those whose works
            the gods have pointed out to us.

143

THE HYMN TO THE MOON

Go on,
  Muses,
and sing the Moon with her big wings,
                            daughters of Zeus,
                                  son of Cronos,
                            in your sweet voices,
                            you technicians
                                of song

          Off her immortal head
              a brightness,
          pointed from heaven,
               encircles earth,
and from this brightness
             great beauty,
and the air
           that was unlighted before
glows
          with her golden crown,
and her rays spring out
when the goddess
             Selene
has washed her beautiful body
in Ocean,
and put on her clothes
            that shine so far
and yoked her flashing horses
          with their strong necks,
and when she speeds these horses on
          in their beautiful hair,
at evening,
in the middle of the month

             Her great orb is full then
and her rays, as she is

increasing,
become brightest

And she becomes
    an assurance
    a sign
            to men

There was once a time
when she made love
        to Zeus
                in bed
She became pregnant
and had a daughter,
        Pandia,
        who had a particular beauty
        among the immortal gods

Greetings, lady
            goddess with white arms
            divine Selene
            kind Selene
                with your beautiful hair

I began with you
but now I will sing
            the fame of those men who are
                    half divine,
            those men whose works
            have been made famous by
            the lovely mouths of singers
                    who are themselves
                    only servants of the Muses

THE HYMN TO THE DIOSCURI

You Muses,
    with your bright eyes,
tell us about the sons of Zeus,
    the Tyndaridae,
    those great children of Leda
    (she who has such beautiful feet):
        Castor
            who tamed horses
        and Pollux
            a man without fault.

Under the peak of that huge hill
            Taygetus,
    she bore them,
        after making love to
        that black cloud, Zeus.
    Her children are saviours
        to men on earth,
        to men on fast ships
        when wind storms pierce
            an implacable sea.
    Then they call out
        from their ships,
    promising
            the sons of great Zeus
    white lambs
            as they move
        forward
            to the prow.
    But a great wind
        and the sea waves
    start
        to submerge their ship until
suddenly
    these two appear

shooting through the air
              on their yellow wings and
immediately
       they calm the blasts
       of these painful winds,
       they abate the waves
       on this surface
              of the white sea.
       They are good signs
       and they are an end
                     to labor.
       And when men see them
              they rejoice,
              they rest from their work
              and their misery.

Hello, Tyndaridae,
       riding
       on your fast horses
Now I will remember you
       in another song.

THE SECOND HYMN TO THE DIOSCURI

Clear Muse,
sing about Castor and Pollux,
        the Tyndaridae
        who were born
        of Olympian Zeus

            The noble Leda bore them
            under that peak
                    Mount Taygetus
            after being seduced
                    in secret
            by the dark cloud that is Zeus

Hello, Tyndaridae,
        riding
        on your fast horses

THE HYMN TO DELIAN APOLLO

I will remember,
I will not forget
Apollo, the Archer.

He goes through this house of Zeus
and he makes the gods tremble.
They get up, they all get up from their seats
when he comes in,
when he pulls back
his bright bow.

Only Leto waits, she waits
alone, next to Zeus
who so enjoys the thunder.
She unstrings the bow,
and closes the quiver.
She takes the equipment
off those powerful shoulders
with her hands, and hangs it
on a gold hook,
against a pillar,
of this, his father's house.
She leads him
over to a seat,
and then she seats him.
It is nectar then
that his father gives him
in a gold cup.
He welcomes his son,
while the other gods
have him sit down there.

And the lady, Leto, is happy,
the son she made
is strong, and an archer.

149

Be happy, Leto,
the children you made
are glorious,
the lord Apollo,
and Artemis,
whose pleasure is in arrows,
you made her in Ortygia,
him in the crags of Delos,
as you lay down on that vast reach
of the Cynthian hill,
close to the palm tree
and the waters of the Inopus.

How then am I to sing about you,
open as you are
to every kind of song?

Everywhere, Phoebus,
all the divisions of song
are directed towards you,
on the mainland
that raises our cattle,
and on the islands.
All the mountain tops please you,
all the promontories
of rising hills,
the rivers heading out to sea,
the beaches and strands
that lean toward the sea,
they all please you.

Am I to sing how Leto first bore you,
the joy of mankind?
lying against Mount Cynthus
on that craggy island
in Delos that the sea surrounds,
while a black wave
on both sides

pushed out onto the land,
in winds that blew in shrill,
and how when you got up
you began your rule
over everyone.
To all the people of Crete,
to the city of Athens,
to the island of Aegina
and Euboea, famous for its ships,
Aegae and Eiresiae
and Peparethus on the sea,
to Thracian Athos
and the high reaches of Pelion,
to Thracian Samos
and the dark hills of Ida,
to Scyros, to Phocaea,
to the steep hill of Autocane,
to that beautiful place, Imbros,
to the inaccessible Lemnos
and to wealthy Lesbos,
the home of Macar
who is a son of Aeolus,
to Chios, the brightest island
that lies in the sea,
to the rocks of Mimas,
to the high reaches of Corycus,
and to that glitter of Claros,
and to the steep hill of Aesagea,
and to wet Samos
and the sheer heights of Mycale,
to Miletos,
to Cos, the city of Meropian men,
to high Cnidos
and windy Carpathos,
to Naxos and Paros
and to rocky Rhenaea—
to all these places
she came, Leto, in labor pains

for the god who shoots so far,
to see if any of these lands
would want to make a home
for her son.

But they were scared,
they all trembled,
none of them,
even the richest of them,
none of them dared take in Phoebus,
until the lady, Leto,
went up to Delos
and spoke these winged words to her,
and addressed her:

"Delos,
if you would be willing
to be the home of my son,
Phoebus Apollo,
if you would be willing
to make a good temple for him,
and nobody else, by the way,
is even going to touch you,
nor do I think
you're going to be big
in cattle and sheep,
you're not going to have
good vintages, you're not
going to produce many plants at all—
but if you have the temple
of Apollo who shoots so far,
all kinds of men will head here,
bringing their hecatombs,
and the great smell of sacrifice
will ascend from here forever,
and you'll feed the people who live here
out of the hands of foreigners—
your own soil, after all,

is not very good."

That is what she said.
And Delos was overjoyed,
and answered her. She said:
"Leto,
the most glorious daughter of great Coeus,
I would receive your child,
the lord who shoots so far,
gladly. It's only too true
that I am terribly hated by people,
but this way I would become
very highly honored.
But there's this saying
that I'm worried about,
and I won't hide it from you, Leto.
They say that Apollo is going to be
very arrogant and lord it over
gods and mortal people
everywhere on earth.
Now what I'm really afraid of,
in my heart and in my mind,
is that as soon as he sees daylight
he'll simply scoff at this island—
I really am, after all, a rocky place—
and then he'll turn me upside down
and push me into the depths of the sea
with his feet, and then
great waves of the ocean
will wash over my head forever.
He'll go away to some other land,
one that will please him,
and there he'll build his temple
and shaded groves.
And then creatures with many feet
will make their lairs in me,
black seals will make their homes in me,
with no worries, for them, at all,

153

because I won't have any people.
But, goddess,
if you would be so bold
as to swear a great oath
that he'll build
a very beautiful temple here first,
one that would be an oracle for men,
then later on he could build temples
and shaded groves
for everybody else, because
he'll certainly be very famous."

That is what Delos said.
And Leto swore
this great oath of the gods:
"Now listen to this,
Earth, and the broad Sky above us,
and Styx, running your water downward,
(this is the biggest,
the most terrible oath
that exists for the blessed gods)
Phoebus will certainly have
his fragrant altar and his precinct
here, forever, and he will honor you
above everybody else."
And when Leto had sworn
and finished her oath,
Delos was very happy indeed
about the birth
of the lord who shoots so far.
But Leto suffered,
for nine days and nine nights
she was subjected to unimaginable pain.
And all the goddesses were there,
all those who were important,
Dione and Rhea
and Ichnaea and Themis
and Amphitrite who groans so loud,
all the immortal ladies

except Hera, with her white arms.
She sat in the halls of Zeus
who gathers the clouds.
Only Eilithyia hadn't heard,
who is herself in charge of a woman's pain.
She was sitting on top of Olympos,
under gold clouds,
a result of Hera's trickery.
Hera kept her away
through envy,
because Leto, with her beautiful hair,
was about to give birth to
a perfect and powerful son.
So they sent Iris
out of that solid island
to go get Eilithyia,
and they promised her
a great necklace
fitted with gold thread
nine cubits long.
And they told Iris
to call her aside
from Hera,
in case Hera might later
discourage her from going
with her talk.

And when Iris,
whose feet are as fast
as the wind,
heard all this,
she started running
and quickly covered
the whole distance,
and when she got to
the home of the gods,
steep Olympos,
right away

she called Eilithyia
out of the hall,
to the door,
and she spoke winged words to her,
everything
that the goddesses who live on Olympos
told her to.
And it cut to the heart
in her dear breast.
And they went away
on feet that were like
shy doves.
And when Eilithyia,
who is in charge of a woman's pain,
reached Delos,
the labor pain seized Leto,
and she yearned to deliver.
She threw her arms
around the palm tree
and knelt on the soft meadow.
The earth laughed underneath her,
and the child jumped out
towards the light.
All the goddesses started cheering.

Then the goddesses washed you,
great Phoebus,
purely, thoroughly,
with good water,
and they wrapped you
in a white cloth
that was new and fine-spun.
And they attached a gold band.
But Apollo,
who carries a gold sword,
was not given his mother's breast.
Instead, Themis,
with her divine hands,

poured nectar and lovely ambrosia.
And Leto was happy,
because the son she made
was strong, and an archer.

And yet, Phoebus,
once you had tasted
that heavenly food,
the gold cords
could no longer hold you,
nor could the bonds
restrain you,
and everything came undone.
And right away
Phoebus Apollo spoke
to the goddesses:
"The lyre and the bent bow
are always going to be loved by me,
and I will reveal to mankind
the exact will of Zeus."
And when he said this,
Phoebus, the god with long hair,
who shoots so far,
started to walk
on the earth that is wide with roads.
And all the goddesses were astonished.
And Delos covered herself
all in gold,
looking at the child
of Zeus and Leto,
and happy because
the god chose her
instead of the other islands,
or the mainland,
to be his home,
and she loved him even more
in her heart,
and she blossomed

157

like a mountain top
in the flowers of its wood.

And you yourself, Apollo,
silver bow,
shooting so far,
you yourself went walking now
on the steep Cynthus,
and you wandered around the islands
and the people in them.
You have many temples,
many shaded groves.
And all the mountain peaks
are dear to you,
all the sheer cliffs
of high mountains,
all the rivers
running to the sea
are loved by you,
but it's in Delos,
Phoebus,
that you really enjoy yourself.
The Ionians in their long robes
assemble there, with their children,
with their shy wives,
for your sake.
And they remember how much
they delight you,
with their boxing and their dancing
and with singing,
whenever they hold their festival.

Somebody who just happened to see
the Ionians gathered there
would think they were immortal,
that they would never die,
because he'd see their grace,
all of them, and it would please his heart

to look at the men there
and the beautifully dressed women,
their fast ships and
their many possessions.
And then there's this wonderful thing too—
whose fame will never perish:
the girls of Delos—the servants of
him who shoots so far—
when they have sung their hymns to Apollo,
and then to Leto and Artemis,
whose pleasure is arrows,
they sing a hymn that recalls
men and women of the past,
and they charm the races of man.
They know how to imitate
the sounds and the chattering
of all mankind.
Each man would think that
he was himself making the sounds,
for their beautiful song
is that carefully put together.

But come now, Apollo and Artemis,
be gracious, and farewell,
all you women.
Remember me later on,
whenever someone of the men of earth
finds himself here, a stranger
who has suffered a lot,
and he says to you,
"O girls,
who is the sweetest man
that comes here
with his songs for you,
who is it
that pleases you the most?"
Then, all together, answer him:
"A blind man,

he lives in rocky Chios,
and all his songs will still be the best
at the end of time."
And we will carry your fame
wherever we go on the earth,
to all the civilized cities of man,
and they will believe, too,
because it is true.
And I will never forget Apollo,
who shoots so far,
singing hymns for Silver Bow,
whom Leto gave birth to,
with her beautiful hair.

THE HYMN TO PYTHIAN APOLLO

The glorious son of Leto
goes to steep Pytho,
playing his hollow lyre,
wearing divine and perfumed clothes.
And his lyre makes a lovely sound
with its gold pick.
And then, like a thought,
he goes to Olympos
from earth, to the house of Zeus
where the other gods
are gathered.
And suddenly the gods
are only concerned with
the lyre and song,
and all together the Muses sing
the divine gifts of the gods,
each one answering the other
with a beautiful voice,
and the suffering of men,
what they have
from the immortal gods,
how they live,
mindless, helpless,
how they can't find
a cure for death
or a defense against age.
And the Graces
with their beautiful hair
and the Seasons, happy,
dance with Harmonia
and Hebe and Aphrodite,
the daughter of Zeus,
holding each others' hands
by the wrist.
And with them

there is someone else
who dances, not badly,
not small either,
but very big in fact
and of a wonderful shape—
it is Artemis,
whose pleasure is arrows,
the sister of Apollo.
And with them, playing,
is Ares, and Argeiphontes,
sharp-eyes. And Phoebus Apollo
plays his lyre, taking big steps
and beautifully.
And a brightness casts about him,
the flashings of his feet
and his carefully woven gown.
And they are delighted
in their great hearts,
Leto, with her gold hair,
and wise Zeus,
as they look upon
their dear son
playing with the immortal gods.

How then am I to sing about you,
open as you are
to every kind of song?
Shall I sing of you as a lover,
and in love-making?
how you went courting
the daughter of Azan,
with Ischys,
whose father has so many horses?
or with Phorbas
who was of the same line as Triops,
or with Ereutheus,
or with Leucippus
and the wife of Leucippus?

162

you on foot,
he with a chariot,
though he was not inferior
to Triops.
Or, Apollo who shoots so far,
how at first you went
all over the earth
looking for a place
for your oracle for mankind?

First you went to Pieria,
coming down from Olympos,
and you passed by sandy Lectus
and Enienae and through the Perrhaebi.
Soon you came to Iolcus
and you went up to Cenaeum
in Euboeia, famous for its ships.
You stood in the Lelantine Plain,
but you didn't like the idea
of building a temple there,
and shaded groves.
So you went across the Euripus,
Apollo who shoots so far,
and you went up the sacred green hill,
and then you went on to Mycalessus
from there, and the grass-bed
of Teumessus. Then you arrived at the home
of Thebes, covered in wood.
Nobody lived in sacred Thebes yet,
and there weren't any paths there yet,
or any roads around the wheat plains
of Thebes yet, just woods.

And yet you went further,
Apollo who shoots so far,
you went to Onchestus,
the glorious grove of Poseidon.
There a colt that is new at the bit

163

and disgusted with pulling
pretty chariots
breathes a moment,
and a good driver hops down
from the running board
and takes to the road.
And then the horses shake
the empty chariot for a while,
now that they're rid of the driver.
But if they break the chariot
in the shaded grove,
people keep the horses
but push over the chariot
and leave it.
This has been the ritual
from the very beginning.
And they pray there to the lord,
but the chariot is taken
as the god's share.

And yet you went further,
Apollo who shoots so far.
You reached the beautiful stream of Cephissus next,
it propels its beautifully flowing water
from Lilaea, and you went over it,
you who work from a distance,
and you passed the numerous towers of Ocalea
to the grassland of Haliartus.

And then you went towards Telphusa,
and that pleasant place there
was right for a temple and a shaded grove.
You got very close to her
and you spoke these words:
"Telphusa, I'm inclined to build
a very beautiful temple here,
an oracle for mankind,
where everybody will always bring

perfect sacrifices, whether they live
in the rich Peloponnesus
or in Europe, or in the islands
that are surrounded by waves,
because they will be looking for oracles.
And I will give out oracles
to all of them, accurate advice too,
I'll give it to them
in my rich temple."

Phoebus Apollo said this,
and started laying out the foundations,
which were wide and very long throughout.
But Telphusa, when she saw this,
she was outraged in her heart
and she said:
"Lord Phoebus,
you who work from a distance,
I have something to say to you,
since you're inclined to build
a very beautiful temple here,
an oracle for mankind,
where everybody will always bring
perfect sacrifices.
I have something to tell you,
and you pay attention.
The noise of fast horses
and the sound of mules
watering themselves at my sacred springs
will always be a nuisance for you,
and some people will prefer
to look at the well-constructed chariots
and at the noise
of these fast-footed horses
than at your great temple
and all the treasures inside.
But, if I can only persuade you—
and you are stronger, lord, than I am,

and better, you have the greatest power of all—
build at Crisa, under the cliff of Parnassus.
No beautiful chariot
will make a racket there,
and there will be no noise
from fast-footed horses
near your beautifully constructed altar.
There the famous tribes of mankind
will bring gifts to you as 'The Healer,'
and it will delight your heart
to receive beautiful sacrifices
from the people who live around there."
She said all this, Telphusa,
so that she alone would be famous
in this land, and not Far-Shooter.
And she convinced Far-Shooter.

And yet you went further,
Apollo who shoots so far,
and you came to the city
of those arrogant men, the Phlegyae,
who live on this earth
in a beautiful glen
near the Cephisian lake
and who don't pay any attention to Zeus.
Then, suddenly, you raced
up to the mountain ridge,
and you reached Crisa
under the snow of Parnassus,
the shoulder of the mountain
turned toward the west,
where a ledge projects overhead,
and a hollow, rough, glen
runs underneath.

There lord Phoebus Apollo
decided to make his lovely temple,
and he said this:

"It's here that I'm inclined
to build a very beautiful temple,
an oracle for mankind,
where everybody will always bring
perfect sacrifices, whether they live
in the rich Peloponnesus
or in Europe, or in the islands
that are surrounded by waves,
because they will be looking for oracles.
And I will give out oracles
to all of them, accurate advice, too,
I'll give it to them
in my rich temple."

And when he had said this,
he started laying out the foundations,
which were wide and very long throughout.
And over these
the sons of Erginus, Trophonius
and Agamedes, who were loved
by the immortal gods,
laid out a stone base.
And the innumerable tribes of men
built the temple out of smooth stone,
to be the subject of song
for all time.

But near this place there was a spring
that was flowing beautifully,
and there the lord, the son of Zeus,
killed the big fat she-dragon,
with his mighty bow.
She was a wild monster
that worked plenty of evil
on the men of earth,
sometimes on the men themselves,
often on their sheep with their thin feet.
She meant bloody misery.

167

She once received from Hera,
who sits on a golden throne,
the dreaded, cruel Typhaon,
and raised him, a sorrow for mankind.
Hera had given him birth once
when she was mad at father Zeus,
when the son of Cronos himself
was giving birth to glorious Athena
in his head. The lady Hera
got angry then, and said this
to the gods who were assembled:
"Listen to me,
all you gods and goddesses,
how Zeus who gathers the clouds
has begun to dishonor me,
after he has made me
his dearly beloved wife.
Without me, he has given birth
to bright-eyed Athena,
who stands out from all the blessed gods.
But my own boy, Hephaestus,
the one I myself gave birth to,
was weak among all the gods,
and his foot was shrivelled,
why it was a disgrace to me,
a shame in heaven,
so I took him in my hands
and threw him out, and he fell
into the deep sea.
The daughter of Nereus, Thetis,
with her silver feet,
took him and brought him up
with her sisters.
I wish she would have done us blessed gods
some other favor!
Well, wicked, crafty,
what do you plan to do now?
How did you dare give birth,

alone, to bright-eyed Athena?
Wouldn't I have given birth for you?
At least I was called your wife
among the gods
who live in this big heaven.
Watch out now that I don't plan
some trouble for you later on:
yes in fact I will plan something,
that a son will be born to me
who will stand out among the immortal gods,
and it won't shame your sacred marriage
or mine. But I won't come to your bed,
I'll go far away from you
and stay with the immortal gods."

She said all this
and went away from the gods,
her heart very angry. The lady Hera,
with her cow-eyes, then prayed,
and struck the ground
with the flat of her hand, and said:
"Listen to me now,
Earth and wide Heaven overhead,
and you Titan gods
who live under the earth
around big Tartarus,
from whom we get both men and gods.
Listen to me now,
all of you, and give me a child
separate from Zeus, and yet one
who isn't any weaker than him
in strength. In fact.
make him stronger than Zeus,
just as Zeus who sees so far
is stronger than Cronos."
She cried this out
and beat the ground
with her thick hand.

And then Earth,
who brings us life,
was moved. And when she saw it,
she was very happy.
And she expected a fulfillment.

From that point on,
for a full year,
she didn't go once
to the bed of wise Zeus.
She didn't even sit
in her elaborate chair,
as she used to do,
giving him good advice.
No, she stayed in her temples,
the lady Hera, with her cow-eyes,
where many people prayed,
and she enjoyed their sacrifices.
But when the months and days
were finished, and the seasons
came and went with the turning year,
she bore something
that didn't resemble the gods,
or humans, at all: she bore
the dreaded, the cruel, Typhaon,
a sorrow for mankind.
Immediately the lady Hera,
with her cow-eyes, took it
and gave it to her (the she-dragon),
bringing one wicked thing to another.
And she received it.
And it used to do
plenty of terrible things
to the famous tribes of mankind.

Whoever encountered the she-dragon,
it was doomsday for him,
until the lord Apollo,

who works from a distance,
shot a strong arrow at her.
And she lay there,
torn with terrible pain,
gasping deeply, and rolling around
on the ground.
She made an incredible, wonderful noise.
She turned over again and again,
constantly, in the wood.
And then life left her,
breathing up blood.
And Phoebus Apollo boasted:
"Rot right there now,
on the ground that feeds man.
You won't live anymore
to be a monstrous evil to humans
who eat the fruit of the earth
that feeds so many, and
who will bring perfect sacrifices here.
Typhoeus won't save you
from hard death,
nor the infamous Chimera,
but right here the black earth
and the bright sun will rot you."
Phoebus said this, gloating over her,
and darkness covered her eyes.
And the sacred power of the sun
rotted her out right there,
which is why the place is called Pytho (rot),
and why they give the lord
the name of Pythian, because it was right there
that the power of the piercing sun
rotted the monster out.

And then Phoebus Apollo
understood in his mind
how that beautifully flowing stream
had deceived him,

and he went for Telphusa, furious,
and he got there fast.
He stood very close to her
and said this:
"Telphusa, you weren't going to deceive my mind
and keep this lovely place
just for your beautifully flowing waters
to go on flowing.
My fame will also come from this place,
and not just yours alone."
Apollo, who works from a distance,
said this, and pushed over a mountain top
along with a rock-slide,
and covered over her streams.
And he made an altar in a shaded grove,
very near the beautifully flowing stream.
And everybody prays to the lord there
by calling him Telphusian,
because he disfigured the streams
of sacred Telphusa.
Then Phoebus Apollo thought over
in his heart who the priests should be
that he would bring in
to serve him in rocky Pytho.
And while he was thinking about it,
he spotted a fast ship on the wine-sea,
in which there were many men,
and good men, Cretans from Minoan Cnossos,
who make sacrifices to the lord
and announce the laws
of Phoebus Apollo with his gold sword,
whatever he says, answering
from his laurel tree in the valley of Parnassus.
They were sailing
in their black ship, for business
and profit, to sandy Pylos,
to the men of Pylos.
But it was Phoebus Apollo

who met them. He jumped into the sea,
like a dolphin, and onto their fast ship,
and he lay there,
a big, frightening monster.
And none of these men thought about it
in their hearts, enough to understand,
and they wanted to throw the dolphin off.
But he kept rocking the black ship
all over, and he rattled the black ship's beams.
So they sat back, scared and silent,
in their ship. And they didn't let go
the cables in their hollow black ship,
and they didn't let out the sail
of their dark-prowed ship, but
they kept sailing, as they had before,
with the ship fastened with ox-rope.
And a fierce south wind
beat their fast ship from behind.
And first they passed by Malea,
and down the Laconian coast
until they came to that city
that is garlanded by the sea,
Taenarum, the land of the Sun,
who makes men happy.
Here the sheep of Lord Sun,
with their thick fleece,
are always eating,
and live in a joyful land.
Here the men wanted to land
their ship, and go ashore,
and think over the great wonder
and see with their eyes
if the monster would stay on the deck
of their hollow ship,
or whether it would jump back
into the salt sea that's so full of fish.
But their well-built ship
did not obey the rudders,

it kept on going
along the rich coast of Peloponnesus,
and lord Apollo, who works from a distance,
guided it easily with his breath.
It plied its way and came to Arena,
and to lovely Argyphia, and to Thryon,
the ford of the Alpheus, and to Aepy,
that is well situated, and to sandy Pylos,
to the men of Pylos. But it went on,
past Cruni and Chalcis,
past Dyme and marvellous Elis,
where the Epei are in power.
And while it was heading for Pherae,
rejoicing in the breeze of Zeus,
the steep mountain of Ithaca
appeared to them beneath the clouds,
and Dulichium and Same
and the woodland Zacynthus.
But when they had passed
the entire Peloponnesus, towards Crisa,
that enormous gulf appeared to them,
which closes off the rich Peloponnesus.
A great west wind came up, clear,
by order of Zeus, blowing furiously
out of the sky, so that the ship
would cease, as soon as possible,
its journey over the salt sea.
And that's when they started sailing back
towards dawn and the sun.
The lord Apollo, son of Zeus,
led them. They reached Crisa,
which you see from a distance,
vine country, and harbor.
Their sea-going ship went aground here
on the sands.

Then the lord Apollo,
who works from a distance,

jumped from the ship,
like a star at mid-day.
Sparks flew off him all over,
and their light reached the sky.
He entered his shrine,
past the tripods,
which were very valuable,
and he made a fire,
revealing his arrows,
and the brightness filled all of Crisa.
And the wives and daughters
of the Crisans, beautifully dressed,
howled at this blast of Phoebus,
for he put great fear in each of them.
And then he leaped out,
like a thought, to speed to the ship again,
in the shape of a man
who is quick and strong,
an adolescent, his wide shoulders
covered with his hair.
He spoke to the men
and said winged words:
"Strangers, who are you?
Where do you come from,
sailing the waterways?
Was it for business
or do you wander recklessly
over the sea, like pirates
who roam around
risking their lives
as they do evil to strangers?
Why do you stand around like this,
grieving, why don't you go ashore,
why don't you put away the gear
of your black ship—which is the custom
among men who eat bread,
whenever they come from the sea
to land, in their black ships,

175

weary with work.
A desire for sweet food
usually seizes their minds right away."
He said this
and put courage in their breasts,
and the leader of the Cretans
answered him back and said:
"Stranger, even though you are not like
ordinary men, neither in your size or shape,
but like the immortal gods,
good health to you and hello,
and may the gods give you
good fortune.
Tell me honestly,
so that I may be sure,
what country is this?
what land? what people live here?
We were thinking of somewhere else
when we went sailing
over the great deep sea
to Pylos, from Crete,
which is where we boast our origin.
And now we've come on our ship here,
not at all willingly,
and we want to return,
we want another route, other paths.
One of the immortal gods
brought us here against our will."
Then Apollo, who works from a distance,
answered them:
"Strangers, you who once lived before this
around the very wooded Cnossos,
you will not be going back again
to the city you love,
or to your beautiful houses,
or to your dear wives. Instead,
you will take care of my rich temple
that is honored by many men.

I am the son of Zeus. I am Apollo.
I brought you here
over the great deep sea.
I intended no evil for you.
Instead, you will take care of my rich temple
that is so honored by all men.
You will get to know
the plans of the gods,
and by their will
you will forever be honored,
on and on through every single day.
But come on, do what I say right now.
First, lower the sails
and set the cables free,
and then pull the fast ship
up on land. Take out your stuff,
and everything in the balanced ship,
and make an altar on the beach of the sea.
Light a fire on it
and offer up white barley
and then stand around the altar
and pray. And since it was as a dolphin
that I first jumped on to your fast ship
in the misty sea, pray to me
as Delphinius. And the altar itself
will be called Delphinius,
as well as All-seeing, forever.
And then eat dinner
by your fast black ship
and pour an offering to the blessed gods
who live on Olympos.
And after you've satisfied your desire
for delicious food, come with me
and sing 'Io Paean,' 'Hail Healer,'
until you get to the place
where you will take care of my rich temple."

Apollo said this.

And the men heard him very well,
and they obeyed him.
First the men lowered the sail,
and set free the cables,
and lowered the mast with the forestays
on the mast-hold. And then the men
went up on the beach of the sea.
They dragged the fast ship
onto land out of the sea, up on the sand,
and they put big props under it.
And they made an altar
on the beach of the sea,
and lit a fire, and made an offering
of white barley, and they prayed,
standing around the altar,
as he told them to.
And then they had dinner
next to their fast black ship
and poured an offering to the blessed gods
who live on Olympos.
And when they had satisfied their desire
for food and drink, they started to go.
The lord Apollo, the son of Zeus,
led them, holding a lyre in his hands,
playing it beautifully,
walking high and nicely.
And the Cretans followed him, dancing,
to Pytho, and they sang 'Io Paean'
just like the paean-singers of Crete,
and like those men in whose breasts
the divine Muse has put
beautifully sounding song.
Not tired at all in their feet,
they approached the ridge, and then,
right away, they reached Parnassus
and that lovely place where they were to live
honored by many men.
He led them, and showed them

his sacred shrine and his rich temple.
But their spirit was moved
in their dear breasts,
and the leader of the Cretans asked him:
"O lord, you brought us here
far from our loved ones
and our fatherland, because
it seemed good in your heart,
how are we to live now?
We have to ask you that.
This place isn't any good for vineyards
and it isn't very desirable for pasture,
to live here very well,
and to serve mankind."

And then Apollo, the son of Zeus,
smiled on them, and said:
"What foolish people you are,
what wretches, that in your hearts
you want trouble, and painful work,
and distress. Now I'm going to tell you something,
something pleasing, and put it in your heads:
Even if each one of you,
with a knife in your hand,
were to kill sheep constantly,
there would still remain
an endless supply, all in fact
that the famous tribes of mankind
bring here for me.
So guard my temple,
and welcome the tribes of mankind
who gather here, and tell them,
most important of all,
what my will is.
And maintain justice in your hearts.
But if any of you is disobedient,
or careless, or contemptuous,
or if there are any idle words
or incidents or arrogance,

179

which is, after all, the custom
among human beings, then other men
will become your masters,
and they will subdue you with force
forever. Now everything has been said.
Guard it in your hearts."

And so, farewell,
son of Zeus and Leto.
But I will remember you
in other hymns.

AFTERWORD

A hymn, or *hymnos*, originally meant a form of "woven" or "spun" speech. Although the etymology is not Greek but Asiatic, the word derives from a Greek word for weaving, *hyphainein*. In fact, the Greek poet Bacchylides, in one of his poems (*Ode V*, 8), speaks of "weaving a hymn." Homer, in the *Iliad*, speaks of Menelaus and Odysseus as having "spun" (*hyphainon*) "their words and their counsels" (III, 212).

In its primal Greek use, a hymn was thought of as what results when you intertwine speech with rhythm and song. And it is in this sense precisely that the word "hymn" appears in its oldest recorded usage, in the *Odyssey*, when Alcinoos invites Odysseus to "enjoy dinner and listen to the spinning of a yarn" (*aoides hymnon*) (VIII, 429).

While this collection is traditionally known as the *Homeric Hymns*, the generic name for them originally was *prooimia* ("preludes" or "preambles"). The Greek poet, Pindar, first used the term *prooimion* to describe the kind of introduction which Homeric poets often used to begin their narratives. Pindar's *Second Nemean Ode* begins:

> Just as the Homeridai,
> the rhapsode singers of stories, for the most part
> start with a prelude to Zeus,
> so also is this man given his first song
> for victory in the sacred Nemean games
> in Zeus' famous grove.

It would be deceptive, though, to think of all the hymns as preludes to presumably longer recitations by the Homeric rhapsodes (though this was the influential view of Friedrich Wolf at the beginning of modern classical scholarship). Today it is generally assumed that only some of the shorter hymns in this collection could have been actual preludes in Pindar's sense. The term *prooimion* probably was meant more in our musical sense of "Prelude"—as a developed form that extends beyond a mere introduction. It has always puzzled readers that the longer hymns could have been mere preludes, since they would probably have been longer in themselves than what they were designed to precede. We have to think of the *Homeric Hymns* as a collection based on both kinds of compositions— some functioning as mere preludes to longer compositions of Homeric material and others functioning as independent compositions (though still called "preludes") recited at contests and festivals. As a genre, the *Homeric Hymns* were perhaps a kind of sideline for the professional poet of the Homeric period.

But who were the poets who composed the *Homeric Hymns?* Only one of them actually names himself—Cynaethus of Chios, who identifies himself as the author of the *Hymn to Delian Apollo*. Pausanias, however, the great Greek geographer and antiquarian tour guide of the second century A.D., gives us the names of five major early hymn-singers, including Homer. These are Olen, Pamphos, Homer, Musaeus, and Orpheus.

Pausanias says that Olen, a Lycian, was the oldest and first hymn-singer. He is quoted as the author of a hymn to Eilithyia about the birth of Apollo and Artemis.

> Boeo, a native woman who composed a hymn
> for the Delphians, said that the oracle
> (at Delphi) was established for the god
> by people who came from the Hyperboreans,
> Olen and others. And that he was the first
> to prophesy and the first to sing the
> hexametre.
> (Pausanias, X, v., 7)

Pausanias names Pamphos, also, as an older hymn-singer than Homer:

> After Olen, Pamphos and Orpheus wrote verses,
> and both of them made poems to Eros, so that
> the Lycomidae would sing them in their rituals.
> I read them after talking to a man who was
> a torchbearer.
> (Pausanias, IX, xxvii, 2)

Orpheus, who also wrote hymns for ritual purposes, is compared by Pausanias to the *Homeric Hymns:*

Whoever has worked on poetry knows that the
hymns of Orpheus are all very short and that
his whole collection is not very big. The
Lycomidae know them and chant them in their
rituals. As far as beauty of verses is concerned,
his would rank second after the hymns of Homer,
though they have been even more honored by
the gods.

(Pausanias, IX, xxx, 12)

Pausanias also describes Musaeus, the author of a hymn to
Demeter, as likewise associated with the cult of the Lycomidae.
Other sources mention other pre-Homeric and contemporary
poets, such as Linus, Thamyris, Philammon, Amphion, Anthes,
and Pierus.

These are references, in most cases, however, to cult-hymns
composed in lyric meter. The *Homeric Hymns* were for the most
part not cult-oriented and were all composed in the hexametre.
There is no real information about Homer from antiquity.
His name was attached to the *Iliad* and the *Odyssey* from the
beginning, and to a few shorter works that suggest his style, as
well as to a few that do not. His oral compositions, as an
aoidos or "singer," were performed for audiences, sometimes at
aristocratic banquets (as shown by the example of Demodocus'
singing in the *Odyssey*), sometimes at large public festivals. Of
the latter, the festival at Delos is a good example, as shown in
the *Homeric Hymn to Delian Apollo*:

The Ionians in their long robes
assemble there [in Delos], with their children,
with their shy wives,
for your sake.
And they remember how much
they delight you,
with their boxing and their dancing
and with singing,
whenever they hold their festival.

(147–150)

While no precise dating is possible, scholars seem agreed
that the probable date of composition of the *Iliad* and the
Odyssey, as we know them, is somewhere in the eighth century
B.C. The oldest of the *Homeric Hymns*, the *Hymn to Delian Apollo*
and the *Hymn to Demeter*, are conventionally dated (on the
basis of linguistic and archaeological evidence) as no later than

650 B.C. (though parts of them may be earlier). They are not the work of the author of the *Iliad* and *Odyssey*, but of his followers in the narrative hexametre, the so called "Homerids."

The *Hymn to Aphrodite* may be as old as the *Hymn to Delian Apollo* and the *Hymn to Demeter*, but the *Hymn to Hermes* is later than the other long hymns, and is probably from the sixth century. The *Hymn to Pan* is no older than the fifth century. The shorter hymns in general seem to belong to the Classical Period. *The Hymns to the Sun and Moon*, on the other hand, probably are as late as the Alexandrian Period.

C.B.

Date Due